A Theory of International Trade under Uncertainty

This is a Volume in
ECONOMIC THEORY, ECONOMETRICS, AND MATHEMATICAL
  ECONOMICS

A Series of Monographs and Textbooks

Consulting Editor: KARL SHELL

A complete list of titles in this series appears at the end of this volume.

A Theory of International Trade under Uncertainty

ELHANAN HELPMAN

ASSAF RAZIN

DEPARTMENT OF ECONOMICS
TEL-AVIV UNIVERSITY
TEL-AVIV, ISRAEL

ACADEMIC PRESS   New York   San Francisco   London   1978
A Subsidiary of Harcourt Brace Jovanovich, Publishers

ACADEMIC PRESS, INC.
111 Fifth Avenue, New York, New York 10003

United Kingdom Edition published by
ACADEMIC PRESS, INC. (LONDON) LTD.
24/28 Oval Road, London NW1   7DX

Library of Congress Cataloging in Publication Data

Helpman, Elhanan.
    A theory of international trade under uncertainty.
    (Economic theory, econometrics, and mathematical
    economics series)
    Includes bibliographies.
    1. International economic relations.
2. Balance of payments.   3. International finance.
I. Razin, Assaf, joint author.   II. Title.
HF1411.H385   382.1'04   78–8837
ISBN 0–12–339650–6

PRINTED IN THE UNITED STATES OF AMERICA

78 79 80 81 82   9 8 7 6 5 4 3 2 1

To my parents
E. H.

In the memory of my father
A. R.

Contents

Preface   xi

Chapter 1
Introduction   1

       References   3

Chapter 2
Elements of the Deterministic Theory of International Trade   5

  2.1 The Ricardian Theory   5
  2.2 The Heckscher–Ohlin Theory   13
       References   26

Chapter 3
**Elements of the Theory of Economic Decision Making
under Uncertainty**   27

  3.1 Expected Utility, Risk Aversion, and Portfolio Choice   27
  3.2 Increasing Risk   31

3.3   Markets for Risk Sharing   32
3.4   Individual Decision Making under Uncertainty: An Application   35
      References   41

Chapter 4

A Critical Survey of the Literature   43

4.1   The General Framework   43
4.2   Ex-Ante Trading Decisions   44
4.3   Ex-Post Commodity Trading Decisions   50
4.4   Financial Markets   58
      References   61

Chapter 5

A Stock Market Economy   63

5.1   The Framework   64
5.2   Firms   65
5.3   Consumers   69
5.4   An Alternative Specification   71
5.5   Equilibrium   73
      References   77

Chapter 6

**A Diagrammatic Exposition of Stock Market Equilibrium
and the Balance of Payments**   79

6.1   The Basic Problems   80
6.2   No International Trade in Securities   81
6.3   International Trade in Securities   86
6.4   Stock Market Equilibrium with a Safe Bond   89
      References   91

Chapter 7

**The Basic Propositions of the Pure Theory of International
Trade Revised**   93

7.1   Comparative Costs Theory   94
7.2   Factor-Price Equalization   99
7.3   The Stolper–Samuelson Theorem   103
7.4   The Rybczynski Theorem   105
7.5   The Heckscher–Ohlin Theorem   106
      References   107

Chapter 8
Commercial Policy   109

    8.1 The Deterministic Model   109
    8.2 Protection under Uncertainty   111
    8.3 Welfare Losses from Tariffs   119
         References   126

Chapter 9
Gains from Trade   127

    9.1 Gains from Trade for a Small Country   127
    9.2 An Improvement in the Terms of Trade   131
    9.3 Gains from Restricted Trade   133
    9.4 Gains from Trade for a Large Country   137
         Reference   137

Chapter 10
Efficient Intervention in Financial Capital Markets   139

    10.1 First-Best Taxation of Equities   139
    10.2 A Second-Best Argument for Equity Taxation   142
    10.3 Optimal Intervention in the Presence of Confiscation Risks   149
         References   155

Chapter 11
A Dynamic Reformulation   157

    11.1 The Model   157
    11.2 A Diagrammatic Exposition   160
    11.3 The Basic Propositions   162
    11.4 An Example   163
         References   171

Appendix A
Derivation of Equation (8.15)   173

Appendix B
Derivation of the Optimal Policies for Section 10.3   177

Index   183

Preface

The literature on international trade has dealt separately with international trade in goods and international financial capital flows, i.e., international trade in securities. These channels of international trade are interrelated, and there are many problems with which one cannot deal in a satisfactory way without explicit recognition of the interactions between them. We develop an integrated general equilibrium framework for the analysis of international trade in goods and securities. This framework recognizes the dependence of markets for goods on financial markets and vice versa. The usefulness of our approach is demonstrated throughout the book by means of applications to questions such as the effects of international trade on resource allocation, tariff policy, and intervention in financial capital markets. We derive new results which are important for theoretical as well as policy oriented applications.

Our study draws mainly on two branches of economics: the theory of international trade and the theory of financial markets. The book is self-contained in that we provide in its early parts appropriate background on relevant material from these fields. It is primarily directed to economists who are interested in international trade or international finance, including graduate students who specialize in these fields.

This study began in 1975 in the Department of Economics and the Foerder Institute of Economic Research at Tel-Aviv University, and it was continued when the first author was visiting the Department of Economics at the University of Rochester and the second author was visiting the Department of Economics at Northwestern University. We wish to thank all these institutions for very helpful cooperation as well as the Ford Foundation for supporting our work on Chapters 8 and 10.

For comments on parts of earlier drafts, we wish to thank Wilfred Ethier, Murray Kemp, Anne Krueger, and John Pomery. Lou Golan provided editorial assistance and Hiroshi Kodaira provided research assistance. For skillful typing we wish to thank Ms. Stella Fedida from the Foerder Institute of Economic Research, Ms. Virginia Bostrom from Northwestern University, and Ms. Martha Colburn and Ms. Marjorie Adams from the University of Rochester.

Portions of this study appear in our papers "Uncertainty and International Trade in the Presence of Stock Markets," *Review of Economic Studies* (June 1978), "Welfare Aspects of International Trade in Goods and Securities," *Quarterly Journal of Economics* (August 1978), and "The Protective Effect of a Tariff under Uncertainty," *Journal of Political Economy* (December 1978).

A Theory of International Trade
under Uncertainty

Chapter 1

Introduction

For many years the main body of the theory of international trade was confined to nonstochastic environments. This is not to say that the importance of uncertainty was not recognized. To the contrary, on many occasions arguments about the existence of uncertainty were used to justify assumptions upon which a deterministic analysis was built. For example, this procedure has been almost standard in the analysis of macroeconomic models, in which it is assumed that the composition of portfolios depends on the expected returns on domestic and foreign assets, but which use models without explicit random elements.

Much of the theory of international capital flows relies on the existence of uncertainty. Following the work of Markowitz (1959) and Tobin (1958) on portfolio selection, studies of international financial capital flows adopted the mean-variance approach, and concentrated on trade in securities without explicit interaction with problems of commodity trade. This resulted in a situation in which the theory of international trade in goods abstracted from trade in securities while the theory of international trade in securities abstracted from trade in goods. This situation continued to prevail even after elements of uncertainty were introduced into the formal theory of international trade in commodities; models that were developed abstracted from trade in securities.

In the present study we develop a theory of international trade in goods and securities in the presence of uncertainty. Our approach makes use of recent developments in the theory of financial markets, which we integrate in a systematic way into the theory of international trade. This approach proves to be fruitful, as we demonstrate by analyzing a series of problems which are intimately related to the interaction between trade in goods and trade in securities, and problems which are related to the impact of trade in securities on the domestic allocation of factors of production.

Thus, we demonstrate in Chapter 7 that many of the fundamental theorems of the theory of international trade carry-over to uncertain environments in the presence of international trade in equities, but that they do not carry over in the absence of international trade in equities. It may prove useful to evaluate this result in the light of the following passage from Kemp (1976, p. 260):

> To anyone who has not himself attempted to reformulate the central theorems of trade theory to accommodate elements of uncertainty it must seem quite extraordinary that such a reformulation has not long ago been provided by others; but no one who has made the attempt will be in the least surprised. The recognition of uncertainty seems to have a devastating effect on many of our most cherished propositions.

In Chapter 8 we show that in the absence of international trade in equities a tariff may provide protection to the exporting industry of a small country, but that this paradoxical possibility does not arise in the presence of international trade in equities. These two examples demonstrate the importance of international trade in securities in the presence of uncertainty, and we expand more on this theme throughout the text.

We have made a special effort to present our results in a way which will make them accessible to a wide audience. We make heavy use of diagrams in order to clarify our arguments, and wherever possible we use well-known diagrams from the deterministic trade literature, while examples are used to demonstrate new results. No heavy mathematics are used; the reader is required to know no more than calculus. It is, however, assumed that the reader knows some theory of production and the theory of consumer behavior. Hence, the book is accessible to graduate students who had a course in microeconomic theory.

In order to make this volume self-contained, we survey in Chapter 2 relevant elements from the theory of international trade, and in Chapter 3 relevant elements from the theory of decision making under uncertainty. Readers who are familiar with these subjects may begin with Chapter 4 which provides a critical survey of the literature of international trade under uncertainty antedating our own work. Then, in Chapter 5, we develop our basic model in a general equilibrium framework. There we also describe the behavior of firms and consumers–investors in an economy with stock markets. Our basic model is presented by means of diagrams in Chapter 6. These diagrams are then used throughout the rest of the book. The fundamental theorems of international trade theory are reformulated in Chapter 7. Problems of commercial policy are discussed in Chapter 8, while gains from trade in goods and securities are discussed in Chapter 9. In Chapter 10 we discuss issues of intervention in financial capital markets, and we conclude with a dynamic extension of our basic model in Chapter 11.

REFERENCES

Kemp, M. C. (1976). "Three Topics in the Theory of International Trade—Distribution, Welfare and Uncertainty." North-Holland Publ., Amsterdam.

Markowitz, H. M. (1959). "Portfolio Selection." Wiley, New York.

Tobin, J. (1958). Liquidity preference as behavior toward risk, *Review of Economic Studies* **25** (February), 65–86.

Chapter 2

Elements of the Deterministic Theory of International Trade

The purpose of this chapter is to briefly survey some of the fundamental elements of the deterministic Ricardian and Heckscher–Ohlin theories of international trade. These elements will be used repeatedly in later chapters in the construction and evaluation of the theory that we develop. This chapter is designed for readers who have studied international trade and need to be reminded of its basic theory, but it may also serve as an introduction for those who are newcomers to the field. Newcomers are advised to read the first three parts of Caves and Jones (1977), including the supplements, which provide an excellent introduction to the subject. The reader may also find useful the treatment of the Heckscher–Ohlin theory in Kemp (1969). Those who are familiar with the Ricardian and Heckscher–Ohlin theories of international trade will find no interest in this chapter.

2.1 THE RICARDIAN THEORY

The Ricardian theory, which is sometimes also called the comparative costs theory, is attributed to the English economist David Ricardo, who published his version of the theory in 1817 [see the late edition of Ricardo (1971)]. The theory is concerned with an explanation of patterns of specialization and trade by means of relative productivity differentials among countries. Ricardo concentrated on the production structure, but later developments of his theory incorporated the role of preferences in the determination of international trade equilibria. We shall present the modern version.

Consider a country that is capable of producing two goods by means of labor. The country is endowed with L units of labor and the production of good i requires a_{Li} units of labor per unit output, $i = 1, 2$; that is, a_{Li} is the constant labor–output ratio in sector i. We may represent the production function of good i by

$$(2.1) \qquad\qquad Q_i = f_i(L_i) = \frac{L_i}{a_{Li}}, \qquad i = 1, 2$$

where L_i is the amount of labor employed in the production of good i and Q_i is output of good i.

Equation (2.1) represents the production function of a single firm or of the entire industry that produces good i. We will refer to it as the production function of the industry, so that L_i will stand for labor employed by industry i.

Assuming that the economy is competitive, producers choose labor inputs so as to maximize profits, taking as given the observed wage rate and commodity prices. Hence, the demand for labor by sector i is the solution to

$$(2.2) \qquad\qquad \text{choose} \quad L_i \geq 0$$

$$\text{to maximize}$$

$$\frac{p_i L_i}{a_{Li}} - w L_i$$

where p_i is the price of good i and w is the wage rate. The solution to (2.2) yields a labor demand function as depicted by the heavy line in Figure 2.1 and an output supply function as depicted by the heavy line in Figure 2.2.

For every pair of commodity prices (p_1, p_2) there exists a unique wage rate at which aggregate labor demand equals the supply of labor. Figure 2.3 shows all possible outcomes: Figure 2.3a for the case

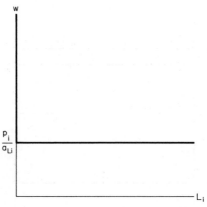

FIGURE 2.1

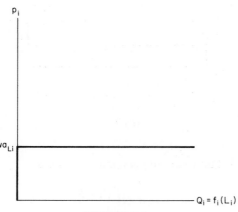

FIGURE 2.2

$p_2/a_{L2} < p_1/a_{L1}$; Figure 2.3b for the case $p_2/a_{L2} = p_1/a_{L1}$; and Figure 2.3c for the case $p_2/a_{L2} > p_1/a_{L1}$.

In Figure 2.3 we measure the labor of the first sector from left to right and that of the second sector from right to left. Hence, the labor–demand curve of the second sector is the mirror image of the demand curve depicted in Figure 2.1. Equilibrium obtains at the point of intersection of the two labor–demand curves, and the equilibrium points are denoted by E. Observe that in Figure 2.3b the horizontal portions of the demand curves coincide, so that all points on the horizontal line constitute an equilibrium. It is clear from Figure 2.3

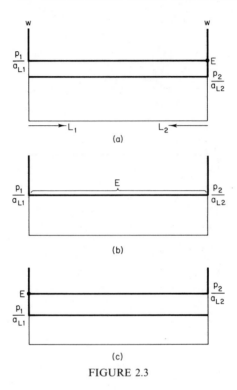

FIGURE 2.3

that the equilibrium wage rate is related to prices by

$$(2.3) \qquad w = \max\left(\frac{p_1}{a_{L1}}, \frac{p_2}{a_{L2}}\right)$$

Observe also that in equilibrium all labor is allocated to the first industry in Figure 2.3a, to the second industry in Figure 2.3c, and that every full employment allocation of labor is consistent with equilibrium in the labor market in Figure 2.3b. Hence, on the supply side

$$(2.4a) \qquad \frac{p_2}{p_1} < \frac{a_{L2}}{a_{L1}} \qquad \text{implies} \quad Q_1 = \frac{L}{a_{L1}} \quad \text{and} \quad Q_2 = 0$$

$$(2.4b) \qquad \frac{p_2}{p_1} = \frac{a_{L2}}{a_{L1}} \qquad \text{implies} \quad Q_1 = \frac{L_1}{a_{L1}} \quad \text{and} \quad Q_2 = \frac{L - L_1}{a_{L2}}$$

$$\text{for all} \quad 0 \le L_1 \le L$$

(2.4c) $\dfrac{p_2}{p_1} > \dfrac{a_{L2}}{a_{L1}}$ implies $Q_1 = 0$ and $Q_2 = \dfrac{L}{a_{L2}}$

The last result can also be represented with the aid of a transformation curve. Since $Q_i = L_i/a_{Li}$, $i = 1, 2$, we have

(2.5) $L_i = a_{Li}Q_i, \qquad i = 1, 2$

Now, using (2.5), the full employment labor constraint $L_1 + L_2 = L$ can be written as

(2.6) $a_{L1}Q_1 + a_{L2}Q_2 = L, \qquad Q_1, Q_2 \geq 0$

Equation (2.6) defines implicitly the transformation curve of the economy. This curve is represented by the straight line TT in Figure 2.4, with the vertical intercept L/a_{L1} and the horizontal intercept L/a_{L2}. The slope of TT (toward the horizontal axis) is a_{L2}/a_{L1}, which is the constant rate at which Q_2 can be transformed into Q_1. In order to see this, make the following experiment. Reduce the output of good 2 by one unit. This will save a_{L2} units of labor. If this labor is applied to the production of good 1, it will produce a_{L2}/a_{L1} units of good 1.

Now, according to Figure 2.3, if the relative price of good 2 (p_2/p_1) is smaller than its relative labor requirement (a_{L2}/a_{L1}, which equals

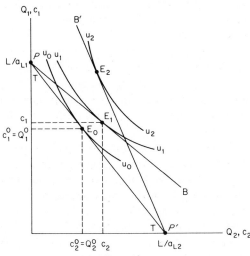

FIGURE 2.4

the slope of the transformation curve TT), then producers will choose to produce at point P in Figure 2.4. If the relative price of good 2 is just equal to its relative labor requirement, then producers will be willing to produce anywhere on the transformation curve. If the relative price of good 2 is larger than its relative labor requirement, then they will choose to produce at P'. These choices are consistent with maximization of national income.

Consumers derive income from sales of labor services. But from (2.3) and (2.4), equilibrium wages are

$$(2.7) \qquad\qquad wL = p_1 Q_1 + p_2 Q_2$$

Hence, the consumers' budget line is

$$(2.8) \qquad\qquad p_1 c_1 + p_2 c_2 = p_1 Q_1 + p_2 Q_2$$

where c_i is consumption of good i, $i = 1, 2$. The slope of this budget line is p_2/p_1 and it passes through the production point in Figure 2.4. Thus, TT is the budget line when $p_2/p_1 = a_{L2}/a_{L1}$, PB is the budget line when $p_2/p_1 < a_{L2}/a_{L1}$, and the slope of PB is p_2/p_1.

Suppose that all individuals are alike; they have the same preferences, labor endowments, and productivity levels. Then, we can draw in Figure 2.4 a set of community indifference curves [see Samuelson (1956) for a discussion of community indifference curves]. The consumption point is chosen on the budget line at a point of tangency between an indifference curve and the budget line. Thus, if $p_2/p_1 < a_{L2}/a_{L1}$, producers choose the production point P (at which $Q_1 = L/a_{L1}$ and $Q_2 = 0$), the budget line is PB (assuming that the slope of PB is p_2/p_1), and the chosen consumption point is E_1. If $p_2/p_1 = a_{L2}/a_{L1}$, the budget line coincides with the transformation curve and the consumption point is E_0. If $p_2/p_1 > a_{L2}/a_{L1}$, the production point is P' and the consumption point is E_2 (assuming that the slope of $P'B'$ is p_2/p_1).

Consider now the situation in which there is no international trade. In this case equilibrium commodity prices are those prices at which the domestic supply of goods equals the domestic demand. This occurs in Figure 2.4 only at the price ratio which equals the domestic marginal rate of transformation; that is, $p_2/p_1 = a_{L2}/a_{L1}$, with consumption and production being at E_0. It is also possible to have equilibrium output and consumption at a corner point such as P or P', with the relative price of good 2 falling short of or exceeding, respectively, the domestic marginal rate of transformation. But even in this case, of a corner equilibrium, $p_2/p_1 = a_{L2}/a_{L1}$ *is* an equilibrium relative price, although not necessarily the unique equilibrium relative price. We shall abstain from further discussing the corner equilibrium in order to concentrate on the main issues.

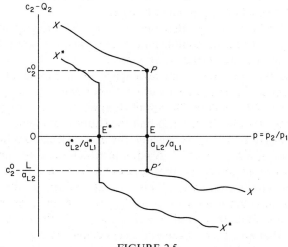

FIGURE 2.5

By changing the relative price p_2/p_1, we trace the excess demand function of the economy for good 2. By using Figure 2.4, and assuming that good 2 is normal in consumption, it is easy to see that the excess demand function for good 2 is as described by the curve XX in Figure 2.5. It is above the horizontal axis and declining to the left of a_{L2}/a_{L1} (where good 2 is imported), and it is below the horizontal axis to the right of a_{L2}/a_{L1}, although it may have there some increasing portions. Point P corresponds to the situation in which at prices a_{L2}/a_{L1} the economy specializes in the production of good 1 (point P in Figure 2.4), while point P' corresponds to the situation in which at prices a_{L2}/a_{L1} the economy specializes in the production of good 2 (point P' in Figure 2.4). Point E corresponds to the situation in which at prices a_{L2}/a_{L1} the economy produces the demanded quantities of both goods (point E_0 in Figure 2.4). Clearly, the equilibrium price ratio is equal to the marginal rate of transformation.

Suppose now that there is also another country of the same type as the country that we have discussed so far; call it the foreign country, and denote its variables by asterisks. Assume also that $a_{L2}^*/a_{L1}^* < a_{L2}/a_{L1}$; that is, the relative labor requirement for commodity 2 is lower in the foreign country than in the home country. In this case we say that the foreign country has a comparative advantage in the production of good 2. This does not mean that $a_{L2}^* < a_{L2}$; that is, the foreign country may produce good 2 with more labor per unit output—all we say is that its relative labor requirement is lower.

Let X^*X^* be the excess demand curve of the foreign country for commodity 2. Then, its equilibrium relative price of good 2 in the absence of international trade is a_{L2}^*/a_{L1}^*.

Suppose that the two countries engage in international trade in commodities under perfect competition. Labor does not move between the countries. What will be the equilibrium relative price of good 2 in the presence of trade? In order to find the equilibrium relative price of good 2, we have to add up (vertically) the excess demand schedules of both countries, XX and X^*X^*. A point at which the combined excess demand schedule intersects the horizontal axis in Figure 2.5 will indicate an equilibrium price. This cannot happen to the right of a_{L2}/a_{L1}, because for every $p_2/p_1 > a_{L2}/a_{L1}$ there is an excess supply of good 2 in both countries. It also cannot happen to the left of a_{L2}^*/a_{L1}^*, because in that area there is general excess demand for good 2. Hence, the equilibrium relative price is bounded above by a_{L2}/a_{L1} and below by a_{L2}^*/a_{L1}^*.

Suppose now that in the presence of international trade the equilibrium price ratio does not reach its predetermined bounds; that is,

$$\frac{a_{L2}^*}{a_{L1}^*} < \frac{p_2}{p_1} < \frac{a_{L2}}{a_{L1}}$$

Then the home country will specialize in the production of good 1 (Figure 2.3a), and by a similar argument the foreign country will specialize in the production of good 2. Hence, every country will specialize in production according to its comparative advantage. Moreover, every country will import the commodity in which it has a comparative disadvantage.

Finally, observe that as long as the domestic relative factor requirement *differs* from the foreign relative factor requirement, at least one country will specialize in production according to its comparative advantage. The other country may not specialize, but if it does not, then the posttrade equilibrium relative price of good 2 equals the marginal rate of transformation of this country.

2.2 THE HECKSCHER–OHLIN THEORY

The Heckscher–Ohlin theory of international trade is attributed to the Swedish economists Eli Heckscher and Bertil Ohlin (Heckscher, 1919; Ohlin, 1933). Contrary to the Ricardian theory which explains international trade by means of productivity differentials among countries, that is, mainly a technological explanation, the Heckscher–Ohlin theory explains international trade by means of differences in relative factor abundance. To this end, the basic Heckscher–Ohlin theory employs the assumption of identical linear homogeneous technologies in all countries and occasionally also identical homothetic preferences in all countries.

Since many propositions of the Heckscher–Ohlin theory are technological in their nature, we start the discussion with a description of the technology. Then, after describing the results which are related to technology and factor availability, we proceed to discuss problems of international trade.

Consider the home country which is capable of producing two goods by means of labor and capital. Its production functions are

$$(2.9) \qquad Q_i = f_i(L_i, K_i), \qquad i = 1, 2$$

where $f_i(\cdot)$ is a concave positively linear homogeneous function with positive first-order derivatives, L_i is labor employed by sector i, K_i is physical capital employed by sector i, and Q_i is output of sector i, $i = 1, 2$. As in the Ricardian model, because of constant returns to scale, we can aggregate all firms in a sector into one unit—the sector. We assume that both factors are essential, which means that no positive output can be produced without using positive quantities of labor and capital.

Given commodity prices p_i, $i = 1, 2$, the wage rate w, and the rental rate on capital r, every sector chooses its output and employment of labor and capital so as to maximize profits:

$$(2.10) \qquad \text{choose} \quad Q_i \text{ and } L_i, K_i \geq 0$$

to maximize

$$p_i Q_i - w L_i - r K_i$$

subject to

$$Q_i = f_i(L_i, K_i)$$

We assume that labor and capital are mobile within the economy.

Due to constant returns to scale, the solution to this problem may be unbounded, and it also can be written in the intensive form

(2.10a)   choose Q_i and $a_{Li}, a_{Ki} \geq 0$

to maximize

$(p_i - wa_{Li} - ra_{Ki})Q_i$

subject to

$1 = f_i(a_{Li}, a_{Ki})$

where $a_{Li} = L_i/Q_i$ is the labor–output ratio and $a_{Ki} = K_i/Q_i$ the capital–output ratio in sector i.

It is clear from (2.10a) that the profit maximizing problem can be solved in the following two stages. First, choose $a_{Li}, a_{Ki} \geq 0$ to minimize unit costs of production; that is,

(2.11)   choose $a_{Li}, a_{Ki} \geq 0$

to minimize

$wa_{Li} + ra_{Ki}$

subject to

$1 = f_i(a_{Li}, a_{Ki})$

Second, compare the minimum unit costs with the commodity price p_i. If unit costs fall short of p_i, the Q_i goes to infinity in order to make infinite profits, and the demand for labor and capital also goes to infinity, provided the solution to (2.11) implies strictly positive input–output ratios. If unit costs are just equal to the price p_i, the supply of Q_i is everything between zero and infinity. Corresponding to every quantity of output there is also a demand for inputs. Finally, if minimum unit costs exceed p_i, output supply as well as factor demands fall to zero.

Let $a_{Li}(w, r)$ and $a_{Ki}(w, r)$ denote the solution to (2.11). Then, the minimum unit-cost function is defined by

(2.12) $C_i(w, r) \equiv a_{Li}(w, r)w + a_{Ki}(w, r)r, \qquad i = 1, 2$

The functions $a_{Li}(\cdot)$, $a_{Ki}(\cdot)$, $i = 1, 2$, are homogeneous of degree zero, and the unit cost functions $C_i(\cdot)$, $i = 1, 2$, are concave and homogeneous of degree one. Moreover, from the envelope theorem,

(2.13a)
$$\frac{\partial C_i(w, r)}{\partial w} = a_{Li}(w, r), \qquad i = 1, 2$$

(2.13b)
$$\frac{\partial C_i(w, r)}{\partial r} = a_{Ki}(w, r), \qquad i = 1, 2$$

It is also easy to see that the labor–output ratios are increasing in the rental rate and decreasing in the wage rate, while the capital–output ratios are decreasing in the rental rate and increasing in the wage rate.

Assume now that for every combination of factor prices the efficient capital–labor ratio of sector 2 exceeds that of sector 1. This need not always be the case, but this assumption is essential in some of the well-known propositions in the Heckscher–Ohlin theory. It is referred to as the assumption of no factor intensity reversals. Thus, we assume

(2.14)
$$\frac{a_{K2}(w, r)}{a_{L2}(w, r)} > \frac{a_{K1}(w, r)}{a_{L1}(w, r)} \qquad \text{for all} \quad w, r > 0$$

It is clear from the preceding discussion that the output supply curve is like the heavy line in Figure 2.6, while the factor demand curves are like the heavy lines in Figure 2.7; Figure 2.7a for labor and Figure 2.7b for capital. $\hat{w}_i(p_i, r)$ is the value of w at which $C_i(w, r) = p_i$, and $\hat{r}_i(p_i, w)$ is the value of r at which $C_i(w, r) = p_i$, for $i = 1, 2$. Now,

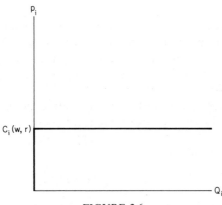

FIGURE 2.6

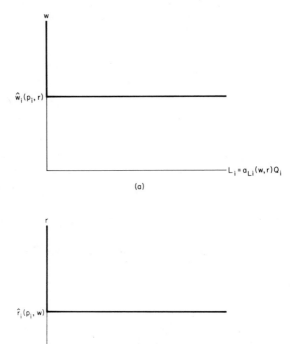

FIGURE 2.7

assuming inelastic supplies of labor and capital, L and K, then given p_i and r, the equilibrium in the labor market can be described by means of Figure 2.8, just as in the Ricardian model (see Figure 2.3). The equilibrium point is denoted by E in every case. A similar figure can be drawn for the market for capital.

Equilibrium in factor markets obtains when factor prices are such that aggregate demand for every factor of production is equal to its supply. Hence, if Q_1 and Q_2 are the supply levels of output, the equilibrium conditions read

(2.15a) $a_{L1}(w, r)Q_1 + a_{L2}(w, r)Q_2 = L$

(2.15b) $a_{K1}(w, r)Q_1 + a_{K2}(w, r)Q_2 = K$

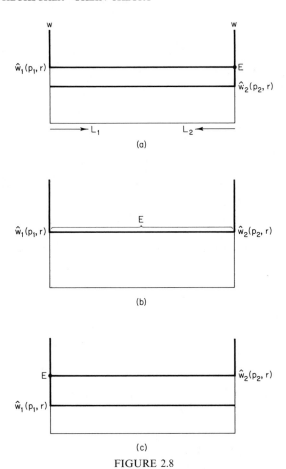

FIGURE 2.8

From the previous discussions it is clear that at equilibrium unit costs cannot fall short of commodity prices, for then there will be an infinite supply of output and an infinite demand for factors of production, which is inconsistent with the factor market equilibrium conditions (2.15) (remember that every factor of production is essential, so that all input–output coefficients are positive). Similarly, the unit-cost functions of both sectors cannot exceed in equilibrium commodity prices, for then the supply of output is zero and so is the demand for every factor of production, which contradicts (2.15). Hence, in equilibrium,

(2.16) $C_i(w, r) \geq p_i$,   with $Q_i = 0$ if $C_i(w, r) > p_i$

and $Q_i \geq 0$ if $C_i(w, r) = p_i$,

$i = 1, 2$,   and strict equality

holding for at least one i

Equations (2.15) and (2.16) describe the production equilibrium conditions in the economy.

Now suppose that equilibrium prices, including factor prices, are such that $Q_i > 0$ for $i = 1, 2$; that is, there is no specialization in production. Then,

(2.17) $$C_i(w, r) = p_i, \qquad i = 1, 2$$

In this case, due to the assumption of no factor intensity reversals, there is a one-to-one correspondence between commodity and factor prices. The relationship between commodity and factor prices is described in Figure 2.9.

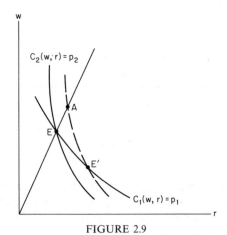

FIGURE 2.9

We have drawn the combinations of factor prices which keep the minimum unit costs of each sector equal to the price of its output. These curves are convex to the origin from the concavity of $C_i(\cdot)$. A slope of such a curve is equal to the capital–labor ratio of the sector, as the reader can verify from (2.13). From the assumption of no factor intensity reversals, these curves can intersect only once, which implies unique equilibrium factor prices for given commodity prices. Hence, there is a one-to-one correspondence between commodity and factor prices for which both sectors just break even. Point E describes an equilibrium for the given commodity prices.

Now suppose that the price of good 2 increases by one percent. Then, the curve of the second sector in Figure 2.9 will shift outward by one percent along any ray from the origin, since $C_2(\cdot)$ is homogeneous of degree one. Let the dashed line represent the new break-even curve of sector 2. Then, the new equilibrium factor prices are described by point E'. It is clear that in this case the wage rate has declined, which means that the reward to labor has also declined in real terms, independently of whether we measure the real reward in terms of good 1, good 2, or a bundle of both goods. It is also clear from the comparison of E' with E that the nominal reward to capital has increased by more than one percent, for point A indicates a one percent increase in the reward to capital and E' is to the right of A. This is called the magnification effect (Jones, 1965). Hence, the real reward to capital has increased in terms of both goods. This proves the Stolper–Samuelson theorem (Stolper and Samuelson, 1941), which states that under the conditions already specified (that is, no factor intensity reversals and incomplete specialization), an increase in the price of a good will induce an increase in the real reward of the factor which is used relatively intensively in the industry which produces this good and a reduction in the real reward of the other factor of production.

Since the unit-cost functions are homogeneous of degree one, this implies that there exist functions $\omega(p_2/p_1)$ and $\rho(p_2/p_1)$, where $\rho(\cdot)$ is increasing and $\omega(\cdot)$ is decreasing, such that for commodity prices in the nonspecialization region

(2.18a) $w = p_1\omega(p_2/p_1)$

(2.18b) $r = p_1\rho(p_2/p_1)$

We have seen that in the case in which the country does not specialize in production, our assumptions assure a one-to-one correspondence between commodity and factor prices. This correspondence depends only on its technology and not on its factor endowments (we will see, however, that factor endowments determine the region of commodity and factor prices within which the country is incompletely specialized). Now, if two countries trade with each other, there are no transportation costs, and no other impediments to trade, then commodity prices will be the same in both countries. As a result, if in the trading equilibrium both countries are incompletely specialized in production and they have identical technologies of the kind already described (including no factor intensity reversals), they will end up with equal factor prices. This is the factor price equalization theorem (Samuelson, 1948).

We turn now to a problem that was considered by Rybczynski (1955). Suppose that the capital stock of a country increases but its commodity prices do not change. How will it affect its output structure?

Suppose, as Rybczynski did, that initially the country does not specialize in production, and that the increase in capital does not induce it to specialize. Then, since commodity prices have not changed, the equilibrium factor prices, which in this case do not depend on factor endowments, also do not change. Hence, producers will not change their input–output ratios. The shift in outputs can be described by means of Figure 2.10 in which we have drawn the combinations of (Q_1, Q_2) which satisfy (2.15a) and (2.15b) (w and r are omitted since they do not change). These are called Rybczynski lines; their intersection, at point E, describes the initial equilibrium output combination. An increase in the capital stock shifts the capital constraint line outward in a parallel fashion, say to the dashed line, and the new equilibrium output combination is described by point E'. Hence, the output of the

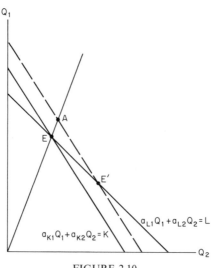

FIGURE 2.10

labor intensive industry, industry 1, declines, and the output of the capital intensive industry increases. Observe, however, that the percentage increase in the output of the capital intensive industry, industry 2, is larger than the percentage increase in the capital stock, because point A describes a proportionate increase in output equal to the proportionate increase in the capital stock, and E' lies to the right of A. This is the magnification effect (Jones, 1965). This impact of a change in the endowment of a factor of production on the output structure is known as the Rybczynski theorem. It states that under the above specified conditions an increase in the endowment of a factor of production increases more than proportionately the output of the industry which uses this factor relatively intensively, and it reduces the output of the other industry.

Consider now the price region in which there is incomplete specialization. This region can be derived as follows. Solve (2.15) for Q_1 and Q_2 to obtain

(2.19a)
$$Q_1 = \frac{L a_{L2}(w, r)}{\Delta(w, r)} \left[\frac{a_{K2}(w, r)}{a_{L2}(w, r)} - \frac{K}{L} \right]$$

(2.19b)
$$Q_2 = \frac{L a_{L1}(w, r)}{\Delta(w, r)} \left[\frac{K}{L} - \frac{a_{K1}(w, r)}{a_{L1}(w, r)} \right]$$

where $\Delta(w, r) \equiv a_{L1}(w, r) a_{K2}(w, r) - a_{L2}(w, r) a_{K1}(w, r) > 0$ for $(w, r) > 0$, due to the factor intensity assumption.

The capital labor ratios $a_{Ki}(w, r)/a_{Li}(w, r)$, $i = 1, 2$, are now functions of only the wage–rental ratio w/r (due to the homogeneity of degree zero of the input–output ratios), and they are increasing in the wage–rental ratio. Therefore, it is clear from (2.19) that there exist lower and upper bounds on the wage–rental ratio, $\underline{\omega}$ and $\bar{\omega}$ respectively, such that Q_1 and Q_2 are positive if and only if the wage–rental ratio is within the open interval $(\underline{\omega}, \bar{\omega})$. This interval defines the factor price region of nonspecialization.

However, nonspecialization also requires unit costs to equal commodity prices, which implies by (2.17) and the homogeneity of degree one of the unit-cost functions that

$$p \equiv \frac{p_2}{p_1} = \frac{C_2(w, r)}{C_1(w, r)} = \frac{C_2(w/r, 1)}{C_2(w/r, 1)} \equiv \xi(w/r)$$

As a result of the Stolper–Samuelson theorem, the function $\xi(\cdot)$ is decreasing in the wage–rental ratio due to our assumption on relative factor intensities. Therefore, defining $\bar{p} \equiv \xi(\underline{\omega})$ and $\underline{p} \equiv \xi(\bar{\omega})$, we have

$$\frac{w}{r} \in (\underline{\omega}, \bar{\omega}) \qquad \text{if and only if} \quad p \in (\underline{p}, \bar{p})$$

The interval $(\underline{p}, \bar{p})$ defines the range of relative commodity prices in which there is incomplete specialization. This interval depends on factor endowments, since $\underline{\omega}$ and $\bar{\omega}$ depend on factor endowments. [See Kemp (1969) for more details on this subject.]

The competitive determination of the output bundle of a country can also be represented by means of a transformation curve. For the Heckscher–Ohlin model with differing intersectoral factor intensities, the transformation curve can be shown to be strictly concave to the origin, such as TT in Figure 2.11. The slope of TT at point A is equal to $\bar{p}$ and the slope of TT at point A' is equal to $\underline{p}$. In a competitive system the economy produces at a point on the transformation curve at which the slope of the transformation curve equals the relative price of good 2, that is, $p = p_2/p_1$ [assuming $p \in (\underline{p}, \bar{p})$]. Through every point on TT we can draw two Rybczynski lines, one for labor and one for capital. For every $p \in (\underline{p}, \bar{p})$ the wage–rental ratio is equal to $\omega(p)/\rho(p)$ [see (2.18)] and this, in turn, determines the employed input–output ratios. Using these coefficients, the chosen output combination on the transformation curve has to satisfy (2.19). We have, therefore,

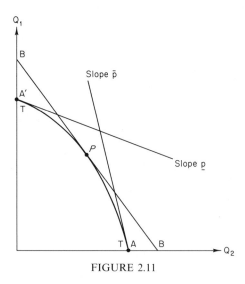

FIGURE 2.11

general-equilibrium supply functions along the transformation curve, which depend on the relative commodity prices and factor endowments, which we can express as

(2.20) $$Q_i = Q_i(p, L, K), \qquad i = 1, 2$$

It is clear that $Q_2(p, L, K)$ increases in K, decreases in L (from the Rybczynski theorem), and increases in p. The function $Q_1(p, L, K)$ decreases in p and K and increases in L.

Due to the homogeneity of degree one of the production functions, competitive factor income equals the value of output and there are no pure profits. Thus, given p which is equal to the slope of line BB in Figure 2.11, the budget line of owners of factors of production is BB, where P is the competitively selected output combination. Aggregating consumers into one unit, as in the previous section, we can draw a set of indifference curves and determine the demand for goods 1 and 2 at the going prices by finding the tangency point between the budget line and the indifference curve. By varying p we can therefore trace the commodity excess demand functions. Assuming that there exists a point of tangency of an indifference curve and the transformation curve with positive outputs of both goods, the excess demand function for commodity 2 looks like XX in Figure 2.12. The autarky equilibrium relative price of good 2 is $\hat{p}$.

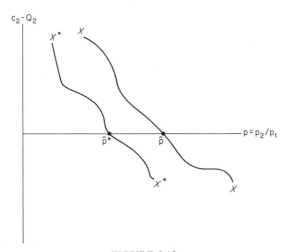

FIGURE 2.12

Suppose that there is also a foreign country whose variables we denote by asterisks. The foreign country is assumed to have the same technology as the home country but possibly different factor endowments. Let X^*X^* in Figure 2.12 be the excess demand by the foreign country for good 2 and let $\hat{p}^*$ be the autarkic relative price for the foreign country of good 2, assumed also to belong to the nonspecialization price interval. Then by the Stolper–Samuelson theorem, the autarkic wage–rental ratio is higher in the foreign country than in the home country. In this case the foreign country is said to be relatively capital abundant according to the Ohlin definition. Ohlin defined relative factor abundance in terms of pretrade relative factor prices (Ohlin, 1933). This is also called the value definition of factor abundance. There is also a quantity definition of factor abundance according to which a country is said to be relatively capital abundant if its endowed capital–labor ratio is higher than in the other country (Jones, 1956–1957).

Now, suppose that the two countries open to international trade. Then, clearly the posttrade equilibrium relative price of good 2 must lie between $\hat{p}^*$ and $\hat{p}$, that is, the relative price of good 2 increases in the foreign country and decreases in the home country. But for any relative price of good 2 between $\hat{p}^*$ and $\hat{p}$, there is an excess demand for good 2 at home and an excess supply of good 2 abroad. This means that the home country imports good 2 and the foreign country imports good 1. Hence, the capital-abundant country according to the value definition of factor abundance, that is, the foreign country, exports the capital intensive good, good 2, while the labor-abundant country, that is, the home country, exports the labor intensive good, good 1. This is the weak version of the Heckscher–Ohlin theorem, which states that a country will export the good whose production is relatively intensive in the relatively abundant factor of production of the country according to the value definition.

The excess demand functions depend not only on the technology and factor endowments but also upon preferences. Hence, the relationship between the pretrade relative commodity prices of the two countries, even when technologies are identical, cannot be uniquely related to relative factor abundance. Therefore, a country which is, say, capital abundant under the value definition is not necessarily capital abundant under the quantity definition. For example, if the foreign country is labor abundant under the quantity definition but its preferences are biased toward good 1, the labor-intensive good, its pretrade relative price of good 2 may be lower than that of the home country, as depicted in Figure 2.12.

If both countries have identical *homothetic* preferences, then a country is capital (labor) abundant under the value definition if and only if it is capital (labor) abundant under the quantity definition. In order to see this, consider Figure 2.13. TT is the transformation curve of the home country and P is its pretrade equilibrium. $\hat{p}$ is given by the slope of BB. Suppose that the foreign country has the same amount of labor but more capital. Then at the relative price $\hat{p}$ foreign producers choose to produce at point P^*, where RR is the Rybczynski line for capital; that is, the labor constraint line. In this case the foreign budget line is B^*B^*, where B^*B^* is parallel to BB and passes through P^*. Since foreigners have the same homothetic preferences as the home country residents, their income–consumption curve (ICC) for the relative price $\hat{p}$ is the ray from the origin which passes through P. Hence they choose to consume at C^*. This means that at the relative price $\hat{p}$ there is an excess supply of good 2 in the foreign country. Therefore, its pretrade equilibrium relative price is lower than $\hat{p}$, which by the Stolper–Samuelson theorem implies that the pretrade wage–rental ratio of the foreign country is higher than that of the home country.

So far we have assumed that both countries have the same amount of labor. But under homothetic preferences the pretrade equilibrium

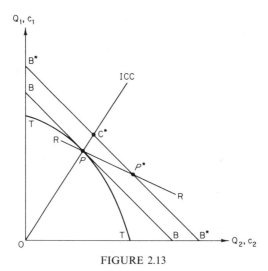

FIGURE 2.13

relative price depends on relative factor abundance but not on their absolute size. Thus, our argument was not restricted to equal labor endowments.

The strong version of the Heckscher–Ohlin theorem can now be stated. Under our assumptions on technologies, if both countries have identical technologies and identical homothetic preferences, a country will export the good whose production is relatively intensive in the factor of production in which that country is relatively abundant under the quantity definition.

This completes our review of the Heckscher–Ohlin theory.

REFERENCES

Caves, R. E., and Jones, R. W. (1977). "World Trade and Payments—An Introduction," 2nd ed. Little, Brown, Boston, Massachusetts.
Heckscher, E. (1919). The effect of foreign trade on the distribution of income, *Ekonomisk Tidscrift* **21**, 497–512, reprinted in "Readings in the Theory of International Trade," Chapter 13. Amer. Econ. Assoc., Philadelphia, Pennsylvania, 1949.
Jones, R. W. (1956–1957). Factor proportions and the Heckscher–Ohlin theorem, *Review of Economic Studies* **24**, 1–10.
Jones, R. W. (1965). The structure of simple general equilibrium models, *Journal of Political Economy* **73**, 557–572.
Kemp, M. C. (1969). "The Pure Theory of International Trade and Investment." Prentice-Hall, Englewood Cliffs, New Jersey.
Ohlin, B. (1933). "Interregional and International Trade." Harvard Univ. Press, Cambridge, Massachusetts.
Ricardo, D. (1971). "The Principles of Political Economy and Taxation." Penguin, New York.
Rybczynski, T. M. (1955). Factor endowment and relative commodity prices, *Economica* **22**, 336–341.
Samuelson, P. A. (1948). International trade and the equalization of factor prices, *Economic Journal* **58**, 163–184.
Samuelson, P. A. (1956). Social indifference curves, *Quarterly Journal of Economics* **70**, 1–22.
Stolper, W. F., and Samuelson, P. A. (1941). Protection and real wages, *Review of Economic Studies* **9**, 58–73.

Chapter 3

Elements of the Theory
of Economic Decision Making
under Uncertainty

In a world of certainty, actions imply in many instances unique consequences. Therefore a choice among consequences determines a choice among actions. However, under uncertainty, an action taken before the resolution of uncertainty does not uniquely determine the outcome. The outcome will also depend on the state of nature that realizes. The meaning of uncertainty is that the individual does not know the state of nature, although he may have a subjective probability belief over states of nature. In this chapter we describe some of the results from the theory of decision making under uncertainty. For the present purpose there can be continuum, countable, or finite states of nature.

3.1 EXPECTED UTILITY, RISK AVERSION, AND PORTFOLIO CHOICE

Assume that it is possible to attach numbers called utilities to consequences of actions in such a way that the *expected utility* measures the desirability of an action (von Neumann and Morgenstern, 1944).

27

A *risk averter* is defined as one who finds it unprofitable to participate in a *fair gamble*. A gamble is said to be fair if its expected value to the individual is zero. Let I and $u(I)$ be, respectively, income and the utility of income. Confronted with a choice among actions, an individual is supposed to choose that action which maximizes the expected utility of income, $Eu(I)$, where E is the expectation operator. No saturation of individual desires implies $u'(I) > 0$, where $u'(I)$ is the marginal utility of income.

Now consider a risk-averse individual who is offered a choice between a certain income I_0 and a chance gamble in which he would gain h_1 with probability π and lose h_2 with probability $1 - \pi$, where h_1 and h_2 are positive numbers. Being a risk averter, if $\pi h_1 - (1 - \pi)h_2 = 0$, he will choose the certain income. If this holds for all h_1, $h_2 > 0$, it implies that $u(\cdot)$ is a concave function of income; that is, $u''(I) < 0$ (see Figure 3.1).

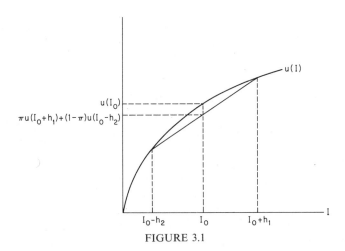

FIGURE 3.1

Arrow (1964) and Pratt (1964) suggested the following risk-aversion measures:

$$A(I) = -\frac{u''(I)}{u'(I)} = \text{absolute risk aversion}$$

$$P(I) = -\frac{Iu''(I)}{u'(I)} = \text{relative risk aversion}$$

where $u''(\cdot)$ is the second derivative of $u(\cdot)$. The measure of absolute (relative) risk aversion is said to be increasing if $A'(I) > 0$ $[P'(I) > 0]$ and it is said to be decreasing if $A'(I) < 0$ $[P'(I) < 0]$.

It can be shown (Arrow, 1964) that if a risk-averse individual is offered a certain income I_0 or a two-state gamble in which he gains h ($h > 0$) in state 1 and loses h in state 2, then for small h he will not be indifferent between the two offers, unless the probability of state 1 exceeds $\frac{1}{2}$ (the probability associated with a fair gamble) by a number which is proportional to $A(I)$. Similarly, if a risk-averse individual is offered a certain income I_0 or a two-state gamble in which he gains hI_0 in state 1 and loses hI_0 in state 2, $h > 0$, then for small h he will not be indifferent between the two offers, unless the probability of the favorable state exceeds $\frac{1}{2}$ by a number which is proportional to $P(I)$.

The following are examples of utility functions with corresponding measures of risk aversion:

(a) $u = 1 - e^{-aI}, \qquad a > 0$

$$\Rightarrow \quad A(I) = a \quad \text{and} \quad P(I) = aI$$

(b) $u = aI - bI^2, \qquad a, b > 0, \qquad \text{for} \quad 0 \le I \le \dfrac{a}{2b},$

$$\Rightarrow \quad A(I) = \frac{2b}{a - 2bI} \quad \text{and} \quad P(I) = \frac{2bI}{a - 2bI}$$

(c) $u = \dfrac{1 - I^{1-a}}{a - 1}, \qquad a \ge 0,$

$$\Rightarrow \quad A(I) = \frac{a}{I} \quad \text{and} \quad P(I) = a$$

The first function exhibits constant absolute and increasing relative risk aversion; the second function exhibits increasing absolute and relative risk aversion; and the third function exhibits decreasing absolute and constant relative risk aversion.

The usefulness of the measures of risk aversion can be seen by considering changes in the optimal portfolio selected by an expected utility maximizer as his initial wealth changes. Consider a risk-averse individual who chooses his portfolio so as to maximize the expected utility of the return on the portfolio. The individual has an initial wealth W_0, which can be allocated between two assets—one safe and one risky. The risky asset yields a return of $R(\alpha)$ in state α, per dollar invested in it. The safe asset yields the same return in every state of nature, which for simplicity will be assumed to be unity. If the individual allocates a fraction s of his initial wealth to the risky asset, his return (income) in state α will be

$$I(\alpha) = W_0 + s[R(\alpha) - 1]W_0$$

Therefore, the investor's problem is

(3.1)   choose s

                    to maximize

$$Eu\{W_0 + s[R(\alpha) - 1]W_0\}$$

If no sign restrictions are imposed on s, the first-order condition for a maximum is

(3.2) $Eu'[I(\alpha)][R(\alpha) - 1] = 0$

We can now show that purchases of the risky asset increase, remain unchanged, or decrease with initial wealth, as there is decreasing, constant, or increasing absolute risk aversion.

To see this define $B = sW_0$ as the total investment in the risky asset, and differentiate (3.2) to obtain

(3.3)
$$\frac{dB}{dW_0} = -\frac{Eu''[I(\alpha)][R(\alpha) - 1]}{Eu''[I(\alpha)][R(\alpha) - 1]^2}$$

By the assumption of risk aversion, the sign of the denominator of (3.3) is negative.

Let $A^* = A(W_0)$ be the value of the absolute risk-aversion measure when the portfolio consists of only the safe asset. The numerator of (3.3) can then be rewritten as

$$Eu''[I(\alpha)][R(\alpha) - 1] = E\frac{u''[I(\alpha)]}{u'[I(\alpha)]} u'[I(\alpha)][R(\alpha) - 1]$$

$$= -EA[I(\alpha)]u'[I(\alpha)][R(\alpha) - 1]$$

$$= E\{A^* - A[I(\alpha)]\}u'[I(\alpha)][R(\alpha) - 1]$$

$$- A^*Eu'[I(\alpha)][R(\alpha) - 1]$$

$$= E\{A(W_0) - A[I(\alpha)]\}u'[I(\alpha)][R(\alpha) - 1]$$

where, in the last step use has been made of (3.2).

If $A'(I) > 0$, then when $R(\alpha) - 1 > 0$, $A(W_0) < A[I(\alpha)]$ and $[R(\alpha) - 1]\{A(W_0) - A[I(\alpha)]\} < 0$; and when $R(\alpha) - 1 < 0$, $A(W_0) > A[I(\alpha)]$, and $[R(\alpha) - 1]\{A(W_0) - A[I(\alpha)]\} < 0$. Therefore, the numerator in (3.3) is negative. Conversely, if $A'(I) < 0$, it can be shown to be positive. If $A'(I) = 0$, the numerator in (3.3) is equal to zero. This proves the assertion.

Analogously, wealth elasticities of the demand for assets are determined by the properties of the measure of relative risk aversion. It can be shown that the wealth elasticity of the demand for the safe asset is greater than, equal to, or less than unity as relative risk aversion is an increasing, constant, or decreasing function of wealth.[1]

Finally, it was shown by Pratt (1964) that a utility function $u^*(\cdot)$ is everywhere more risk averse than a utility function $u(\cdot)$ if and only if $u^*(\cdot)$ is a concave increasing transformation of $u(\cdot)$. This is equivalent to the statement that the absolute (relative) measure of risk aversion is everywhere larger for $u^*(\cdot)$ than for $u(\cdot)$.

3.2 INCREASING RISK

When is an investment venture said to be more risky than another investment venture? Rothschild and Stiglitz (1970) suggest three answers to this question. Let $R(\alpha)$ and $R'(\alpha)$ be random returns on two different investment projects. $R(\alpha)$ is said to be more risky than $R'(\alpha)$ if

(1) $R(\alpha)$ is equal to $R'(\alpha)$ plus some uncorrelated noise, that is, $R(\alpha) = R'(\alpha) + Z(\alpha)$, where $E[Z(\alpha)|R'(\alpha')] = 0$ for all α'.

(2)   Given $ER'(\alpha) \geq ER(\alpha)$, every risk averter prefers $R'(\alpha)$ to $R(\alpha)$ that is, $Eu[R'(\alpha)] \geq Eu[R(\alpha)]$ for all concave $u(\cdot)$.

(3) $R(\alpha)$ and $R'(\alpha)$ have the same mean and $R(\alpha)$ has more weight in the tails than $R'(\alpha)$.

They proved that conditions (1)–(3) lead to a single definition of greater riskiness; that is, conditions (1)–(3) are equivalent. When we deal in Chapter 4 with increasing riskiness, we shall mean mean-preserving transformations of the original distribution, as in (3), which is also equivalent to the other two definitions of increasing riskiness just mentioned.

---

[1] See Arrow (1964). For an analysis of wealth effects on portfolios with more than two assets, see Cass and Stiglitz (1972).

3.3 MARKETS FOR RISK SHARING

A. Contingent Commodity Markets

Imagine an economy which consists of H individuals, and in which there are N commodities and S states of nature. In this economy, trading takes place before the resolution of uncertainty, and individuals can contract on the delivery of every good contingent upon the realization of a state of nature. Thus, if individual h buys 10 units of good 2 contingent on state 7, then he will get the 10 units of good 2 if state 7 realizes, and he will get nothing if another state of nature realizes.

Let $e_i{}^h(\alpha)$ be h's endowment of good i in state α, $c_i{}^h(\alpha)$ be his consumption of good i in state α, and $c^h(\alpha)$ his consumption vector. Then, given contingent commodity prices $g_i(\alpha)$, where $g_i(\alpha)$ is the unit price of good i to be delivered in state α, his budget constraint is

$$(3.4) \qquad \sum_{\alpha=1}^{S} \sum_{i=1}^{N} g_i(\alpha)c_i{}^h(\alpha) \leq \sum_{\alpha=1}^{S} \sum_{i=1}^{N} g_i(\alpha)e_i{}^h(\alpha),$$

$$h = 1, 2, \ldots, H$$

Individual h's tastes are represented by a von Neumann–Morgenstern utility function $u^h(\cdot)$, defined on the consumption vector at that state $c^h(\alpha)$ and the individual's probability beliefs, represented by a vector

$$[\pi^h(1), \pi^h(2), \ldots, \pi^h(S)], \pi^h(\alpha) \geq 0, \qquad \sum_{\alpha=1}^{S} \pi^h(\alpha) = 1$$

where $\pi^h(\alpha)$ is individual h's subjective probability assessment of state α. Let $u^h[c^h(\alpha)]$ be a concave function; that is, $u^h(\cdot)$ exhibits risk aversion. Expected utility of individual h, W^h, is a function of the contingent consumption vector $[c^h(1), c^h(2), \ldots, c^h(S)]$:

$$(3.5) \qquad W^h[c^h(1), c^h(2), \ldots, c^h(S)] = \sum_{\alpha=1}^{S} \pi^h(\alpha)u^h[c^h(\alpha)]$$

Individual h's decision-making problem is to choose the vector of contingent commodity claims $[c^h(1), c^h(2), \ldots, c^h(S)]$ to maximize (3.5) subject to the budget constraint (3.4).

In equilibrium, aggregate demand for every contingent commodity claim has to equal its supply. Namely,

$$(3.6) \qquad \sum_{h=1}^{H} c_i^h(\alpha) = \sum_{h=1}^{H} e_i^h(\alpha),$$

$$i = 1, 2, \ldots, N, \quad \alpha = 1, 2, \ldots, S$$

This is exactly analogous to the certainty case. Note, however, that the number of goods in the uncertainty model is SN instead of N in the certainty model, since here a good is distinguished by the state in which it is consumed in addition to its physical characteristics.

B. Arrow Securities

Instead of markets for commodity claims, assume now that there are securities which are payable in money. The amount of money paid by a security depends on the state of nature that realizes. Security α pays 1 dollar if state α occurs or zero if a different state occurs. There are precisely S such securities. Trade in securities takes place at the beginning of the period. Then, when a state α occurs, trade in commodities takes place.

Let $q(\alpha)$ be the price of security α, and $p_i(\alpha)$ the price of commodity i in state α. Consumer h solves a two-stage decision-making problem. In the first stage, before the resolution of uncertainty, he determines his portfolio; in the second stage, after the resolution of uncertainty, he uses portfolio returns to purchase commodities.

Suppose, for the moment, that the portfolio allocation $[A^h(1),$ $A^h(2), \ldots, A^h(S)]$ has been chosen by individual h, where $A^h(\alpha)$ is his amount of security α holdings, $\alpha = 1, 2, \ldots, S$. Then, when the state of nature α realizes, commodity prices $[p_1(\alpha), \ldots, p_N(\alpha)]$ become known. In state α individual h solves the ordinary consumption problem:

$$(3.7) \qquad \text{choose} \quad c_1^h(\alpha), c_2^h(\alpha), \ldots, c_N^h(\alpha) \geq 0$$

to maximize

$$u^h[c^h(\alpha)]$$

subject to

$$\sum_{i=1}^{N} p_i(\alpha) c_i^h(\alpha) \leq A^h(\alpha)$$

Note that only holdings of security α provide income in state α. The solution to this problem yields the indirect utility function $v^h[p_1(\alpha), \ldots, p_N(\alpha); A^h(\alpha)]$.

Turning to portfolio decisions, individual h chooses $[A^h(1), \ldots, A^h(S)]$ so as to maximize the expected value of his indirect utility function:

(3.8)   choose $A^h(1), A^h(2), \ldots, A^h(S)$

to maximize

$$\sum_{\alpha=1}^{S} \pi^h(\alpha) v^h[p_1(\alpha), \ldots, p_N(\alpha); A^h(\alpha)]$$

subject to

$$\sum_{\alpha=1}^{S} q(\alpha) A^h(\alpha) \leq \sum_{\alpha=1}^{S} q(\alpha) \left[\sum_{i=1}^{N} p_i^h(\alpha) e_i^h(\alpha) \right]$$

where $\sum_{i=1}^{N} p_i(\alpha) e_i^h(\alpha)$ is h's endowment of security α, and it equals the value of his commodity endowment in state α.

In equilibrium the demand for good i in state α equals its supply. Hence,

(3.9) $$\sum_{h=1}^{H} c_i^h(\alpha) = \sum_{h=1}^{H} e_i^h(\alpha),$$

$$i = 1, 2, \ldots, N, \quad \alpha = 1, 2, \ldots, S$$

In addition, the demand for every security equals its supply. Hence,

(3.10) $$\sum_{h=1}^{H} A^h(\alpha) = \sum_{h=1}^{H} \sum_{i=1}^{N} p_i(\alpha) e_i^h(\alpha), \qquad \alpha = 1, 2, \ldots, S$$

To see the relationship between the contingent commodity claims and the Arrow securities models, suppose that

(3.11) $$q(\alpha) p_i(\alpha) = g_i(\alpha)$$

In words, the price of security α times the spot price of commodity i in state α is equal to the price of a claim on one unit of commodity i in state α.

An individual facing those prices has the same opportunities under the two systems. In the securities framework he can effectively acquire a claim to a unit of commodity i in state α by paying $p_i(\alpha) q(\alpha)$. In the contingent commodity claims framework he can effectively acquire a unit of commodity i in state α by paying $g_i(\alpha)$. Hence, the effective price of a unit of a good in a given state is the same under both systems.

Arrow (1963–1964) showed that any Pareto optimal allocation can be realized by either a system of perfectly competitive markets in contingent claims on commodities or by a system of perfectly competitive markets in Arrow securities, provided there are self-fulfilling price expectations. In the former case there are NS markets, while in the latter case there are only $N + S$ markets. The two systems will be referred to as *complete market systems.*

In a complete market system the existing markets reveal an objective price for every good in every state of nature. This price is used by all market participants to evaluate goods in states of nature. If there is production, firms can use these prices to evaluate inputs and outputs so that they can maximize profits as in the deterministic environment. In such cases, producers do not bear risks; risks are borne only by consumers.

Now, one may have a complete market system even if there are no Arrow-type securities. What is important is to have sufficiently diverse securities in adequate numbers so that by an appropriate combination of these securities an investor will be able to assure himself of a dollar return in a particular state of nature and zero return in all other states, for all states of nature. Put differently, if the existing securities are capable of replicating the return patterns of Arrow-type securities, then we have a complete market system. This occurs if there exist S securities with independent patterns of return (in the algebraic sense).

In the real world, however, there are not enough securities to generate complete markets. We have stock markets, bond markets, etc., but the total number of traded securities falls short of the number of states of nature and the economy operates with less than complete markets.

3.4 INDIVIDUAL DECISION MAKING UNDER UNCERTAINTY: AN APPLICATION

In this section we elaborate on some elements of decision making under uncertainty in order to clarify some issues that were discussed in previous sections in general terms. Consider a simplified economy, with a single good, two firms, and two states of nature. A firm produces a state-dependent output with no input, so that the firm faces no decision problem. The firms are owned by individuals, and individuals trade in ownership shares before the resolution of uncertainty. After the resolution of uncertainty there is no incentive to trade in goods, because there is only one good.

We concentrate on a single individual and shall omit, therefore, the superscript. Since there is only one commodity, we also omit the subscript i.

The individual's preferences over consumption in different states of nature are represented by

$$(3.12) \qquad W[c(1), c(2)] = \pi(1)u[c(1)] + \pi(2)u[c(2)]$$

The construction of indifference curves between $c(1)$ and $c(2)$ is shown in Figure 3.2.

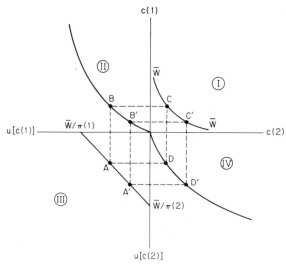

FIGURE 3.2

Quadrants II and IV in Figure 3.2 depict utility as a function of state-1 and state-2 consumptions, respectively. The line ranging from $\bar{W}/\pi(1)$ to $\bar{W}/\pi(2)$ in quadrant III describes all combinations of state-1 and state-2 utility levels for which the level of expected utility is fixed and equal to $\bar{W}$. Point A, in quadrant III, represents one such combination. Point C in quadrant I represents the combination of $c(1)$ and $c(2)$ which corresponds to point A. The same expected utility level is also achieved from the combination which is represented by points A' and C'. Concavity of the utility function implies that the indifference curve $\bar{W}W$ in quadrant I, which connects points C and C', is convex to the origin. This shows that the preference function $W(\cdot)$ has convex to the origin indifference curves.

We turn now to the consumer's opportunity set. Let V_f be the market value of firm f, and let $R_f(\alpha)$ be its return (output) in state α, $f = 1, 2$. At the beginning of the period, V_f is known by every trader in the stock market but $R_f(\alpha)$ is unknown. $R_f(\alpha)$ is known only after the resolution of uncertainty at the end of the period.

At the beginning of the period the consumer buys or sells proportionate shareholdings in firm f at its going market value V_f. We denote by $\bar{s}_f$ his initial share ownership and by s_f his final share ownership in firm f. His portfolio investment is subject to the constraint

$$(3.13) \qquad \sum_{f=1}^{2} s_f V_f = \sum_{f=1}^{2} \bar{s}_f V_f \equiv \bar{V}$$

The individual's consumption in state α equals the return on his portfolio; that is,

$$(3.14) \qquad c(\alpha) = \sum_{f=1}^{2} s_f R_f(\alpha), \qquad \alpha = 1, 2$$

Suppose that it is possible to sell short the ownership shares in firms. For our purposes a short sale is defined as an exchange in which an individual borrows units of a financial asset at the beginning of the period, agreeing to repay the lender the market value of these units at the end of the period. Thus, short sales of firm f shares mean $s_f < 0$.

In order to describe the consumer's two-dimensional opportunity set in consumption space, eliminate the s_f's from (3.14) and substitute them into (3.13) to obtain

$$(3.15) \qquad c(1)\left[\frac{R_2(2)}{V_2} - \frac{R_1(2)}{V_1}\right] + c(2)\left[\frac{R_1(1)}{V_1} - \frac{R_2(1)}{V_2}\right]$$
$$= \frac{[R_1(1)R_2(2) - R_1(2)R_2(1)]\bar{V}}{V_1 V_2}$$

Observe that in an equilibrium all terms in brackets have to be of the same sign. For suppose $R_2(2)/V_2 > R_1(2)/V_1$ and $R_2(1)/V_2 > R_1(1)/V_1$. Then shares of the second firm dominate the shares of the first firm as portfolio assets and there will be an excess demand for type-2 securities. Similarly, if the opposite inequalities hold, there will be an excess demand for type-1 securities. Hence, the terms in brackets on the left-hand side of (3.15) have the same sign. Now,

$$\frac{R_2(2)}{V_2} \geq \frac{R_1(2)}{V_1}$$

$$\frac{R_1(1)}{V_1} \geq \frac{R_2(1)}{V_2}$$

imply

$$R_1(1)R_2(2) \geq R_1(2)R_2(1)$$

and

$$\frac{R_2(2)}{V_2} \leq \frac{R_1(2)}{V_1}$$

$$\frac{R_1(1)}{V_1} \leq \frac{R_2(1)}{V_2}$$

imply

$$R_1(1)R_2(2) \leq R_1(2)R_2(1)$$

Hence, the terms in the brackets are all of the same sign. In the limiting case in which the vectors of returns are linearly dependent, all the terms in brackets are zero.

Assuming linear independence of the vectors of return, the consumption opportunity line described by (3.15) can be represented in Figure 3.3 by line A_1A_2.

Point a represents the bundle which obtains from a portfolio with zero holdings of firm-2 shares; that is, $s_2 = 0$ and $s_1 = \bar{V}/V_1$, while point b represents the bundle which obtains from a portfolio with zero holdings of firm-1 shares; that is, $s_1 = 0$ and $s_2 = \bar{V}/V_2$. The line segment which lies strictly between a and b represents portfolios with positive holdings of firm-1 and firm-2 shares; that is, $s_1 > 0$ and $s_2 > 0$, while points on the line segments aA_1 and bA_2 (excluding a and b) represent portfolios which include short sales of shares in firm-2 and firm-1, respectively.

It is seen from Figure 3.3 that with linearly independent patterns of returns across states and short selling, the consumer's opportunity set

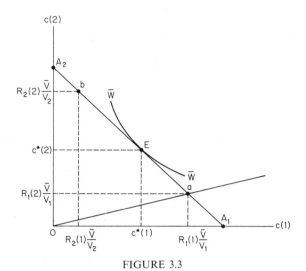

FIGURE 3.3

is $0A_1A_2$ for a given initial wealth $\bar{V}$. By increasing $\bar{V}$ to infinity, the entire nonnegative quadrant becomes the consumption opportunity set. This is equivalent to a situation of complete markets.

Now, if the pattern of returns is linearly dependent, that is, $R_1(1)R_2(2) - R_1(2)R_2(1) = 0$, then line A_1A_2 shrinks to a point, such as point a, and the investor's opportunity set with wealth $\bar{V}$ becomes the line segment $0a$. By increasing his wealth to infinity, his opportunity set becomes the ray from the origin passing through point a. This is a case of incomplete markets. Even by abandoning the assets–budget constraint, an investor is not able to obtain every combination of consumption; there are not sufficient market instruments to achieve it. In this case we have, in fact, only one type of security and two states of nature. Hence, there are too few types of securities compared with the number of states of nature in order to enable equivalence with contingent commodity markets.

Returning to the assumption of linear independence, the consumer's solution is represented by point E in Figure 3.3. The highest achievable expected utility level is shown by the indifference curve $\bar{W}\bar{W}$ and the maximizing expected utility bundle of state-1 and state-2 consumption levels is given by $[c^*(1), c^*(2)]$. The corresponding values of shares in firms 1 and 2, s_1^* and s_2^*, can be determined from (3.14) by substituting $c^*(1)$ and $c^*(2)$ for $c(1)$ and $c(2)$, and solving for s_1 and s_2.

In order to gain more insight, an alternative way of representing the investor's decision-making problem is now discussed. By substituting (3.14) into (3.12), the level of expected utility can be expressed as a function of proportionate shareholdings:

$$(3.16) \qquad U(s_1, s_2) \equiv W\left[\sum_{f=1}^{2} s_f R_f(1),\ \sum_{f=1}^{2} s_f R_f(2) \right]$$

The consumer's preferences over ownership shares in firms can be represented by assets–indifference curves. Since $W(\cdot)$ is concave, $U(\cdot)$ is concave in (s_1, s_2), and we can draw a set of indifference curves between the s_f's, which are convex to the origin.

A typical assets–indifference curve $\bar{U}\bar{U}$ is depicted in Figure 3.4. A similar indifference curve can be drawn even when the number of states of nature is larger than 2, while the number of firms is just 2. Thus, when two firms exist, Figure 3.4 accommodates also various situations of *incomplete markets*.

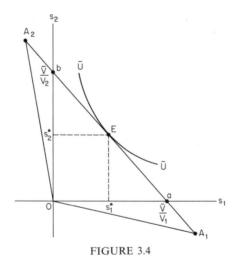

FIGURE 3.4

The opportunity set is described by $0A_2A_1$. The line segment ab describes all affordable combinations of s_1 and s_2 with $s_1 \geq 0$ and $s_2 \geq 0$ on the boundary of this set. It corresponds to the line segment ab in Figure 3.3. If the consumer is short in type-2 assets, that is, $s_2 < 0$, he must use his return on type-1 assets at the end of the period in order to make good his obligation to repay owners of firm 2. Line $0A_1$

describes all combinations of s_1 and s_2 at which $s_2 < 0$, and the consumer is just solvent at the end of the period in an adverse state, say state 2, where the slope of $0A_1$ is $R_1(2)/R_2(2) = \min_i[R_1(i)/R_2(i)]$. Beyond point A_1, along the extension of the line A_2A_1, the consumer cannot fulfill his contract in an adverse state. Similarly, the maximum nonbankrupt amount of short sales of firm-1 assets is indicated by point A_2. The line segments aA_1 and bA_2 in Figure 3.4 correspond to the line segments aA_1 and bA_2 in Figure 3.3.

A typical solution to the consumer decision-making problem is represented by point E in Figure 3.4. At this point the assets–indifference curve $\bar{U}\bar{U}$ is tangent to the budget line A_1A_2. The expected utility maximizing values of shareholdings in firm 1 and firm 2 are given by $s_1{}^*$ and $s_2{}^*$.

REFERENCES

Arrow, K. J. (1963–1964). The role of securities in the optimal allocation of risk bearing, *Review of Economic Studies* **31**, 91–96.
Arrow, K. J. (1964). "Aspects of the Theory of Risk-Bearing." Yrgö Jahnssonin säätio, Helsinki.
Cass, D., and Stiglitz, J. E. (1972). Risk aversion and wealth effects on portfolios with many assets, *Review of Economic Studies* **39**, 331–354.
Pratt, J. W. (1964). Risk aversion in the small and in the large, *Econometrica* **32**, 122–136.
Rothschild, M., and Stiglitz, J. E. (1970). Increasing risk: I. A definition, *Journal of Economic Theory* **2**, 225–243.
von Neumann, J., and Morgenstern, O. (1944). "Theory of Games and Economic Behavior." Princeton Univ. Press, Princeton, New Jersey.

Chapter 4

A Critical Survey of the Literature

For many years, the theory of international trade disregarded elements of uncertainty—even though it was recognized that such elements play an important role in reality. In particular, until very recently, no systematic analysis was made of the impact of uncertainty on trade and specialization. The pioneering work in this field was a 1968 paper by William Brainard and Richard Cooper. From that time (although with some lag), the literature on trade and uncertainty has expanded substantially, and it is still a very active field of research.

This chapter surveys a large part of the literature on uncertainty and international trade antedating our own work. It is not intended to be exhaustive, but is a selective survey in which we discuss works related to our own work, and results which we consider to be of interest. This prepares the ground for a discussion of the approach to be presented in the following chapters.

4.1 THE GENERAL FRAMEWORK

The first studies in this field did not consider financial markets, and many of them were planning models rather than market models.

Three types of uncertainty are considered in the literature: in prices, in technology, and in preferences. In addition, two types of trading decisions are considered: ex ante and ex post. In the ex-ante trading models, trading decisions (exports or imports) are made before the resolution of uncertainty. In particular, these models assume price uncertainty; when an export or import commitment is made, the price which will be paid or received is unknown. In the ex-post trading models, trading decisions are made after uncertainty resolves.

In both types of models, input decisions are made before the resolution of uncertainty. This means that in the presence of technological uncertainty, inputs do not determine a *certain* output level but rather a *distribution* of output.

The following discussion is divided into two parts: ex-ante trading decision models and ex-post trading decision models. In a final section, we discuss recent contributions which discuss financial markets.

4.2   EX-ANTE TRADING DECISIONS

Four papers deal with ex-ante trading decisions (in which export or import decisions are made before the resolution of uncertainty in prices or technology): Brainard and Cooper (1968), Bardhan (1971), Batra and Russell (1974), and Ruffin (1974a).

The general formulation of the problem in the first three papers is as follows. Consider a country which produces and consumes two goods whose outputs we denote by Q_1 and Q_2. Let x be the amount of export of the first commodity. Then, imports of the second commodity are x/p, where p is the relative price of the second commodity in terms of the first commodity. Hence, consumption of the first and second commodities is $c_1 = Q_1 - x$ and $c_2 = Q_2 + x/p$, respectively.

There is a von Neuman–Morgenstern utility function $u(c_1, c_2)$ which exhibits aversion to risk; that is, $u(\cdot)$ is concave. [Brainard and Cooper (1968) assume that $u(\cdot)$ is a quadratic function.]

The technology is represented by a transformation curve $Q_1 = F(Q_2)$. Production and export decisions are made before the state of the world is known. All authors assume that the relative price p is subject to uncertainty, that its distribution is given to the economy under con-

sideration by the rest of the world, and (in most cases) that the transformation curve is nonrandom.

Denoting the relative price of the second commodity in state α by
$p(\alpha)$, the choice problem of the country is

(4.1)   choose Q_1, Q_2 and x

to maximize

$$Eu\left[Q_1 - x, Q_2 + \frac{x}{p(\alpha)}\right]$$

subject to

$$(Q_1, Q_2) \in P$$

where P is an appropriately defined set.

In the formulation of Brainard and Cooper (1968) and Bardhan
(1971), P is simply the transformation curve; in this case, the production
decisions are consistent with the utility function which is maximized.
Batra and Russell (1974) assume that production decisions are made
by maximization of expected national income, which implies that the
economy chooses a point on the transformation curve at which the
marginal rate of transformation between the second and the first
commodities is equal to the expected value of p; in this case, P consists
of this single point only. Obviously, this implies that production decisions are not necessarily consistent with the utility function that is
maximized, which seems to be an undesirable feature of their model
[see also Kemp and Ohyama (1978) on this point].

The major conclusion reached by Brainard and Cooper (1968) and
Bardhan (1971) is that increased uncertainty results in less production
of the export good; that is, more diversification in production. The
mean-variance model of Brainard and Cooper (1968) also implies that
more uncertainty results in less exports.

Batra and Russell (1974) found that more uncertainty reduces the
level of welfare (that is, the level of expected utility). This implies that
if the opening of a country to international trade also exposes it to
larger uncertainty, free trade may be worse than complete autarky.
The optimal policies suggested by them are

(1)   price stabilization by the government to keep the consumer
      relative price $1/p(\alpha)$ constant at the mean of its distribution; or

(2)   a consumption subsidy to the import commodity in order to increase its consumption.[1]

Batra and Russell (1974) can be criticized on two levels: general criticism that applies to the entire class of models described in (4.1), and criticism specific to their model. Let us begin with the latter.

Their conclusions that government intervention is needed and that complete autarky is preferable to trade with a foreign price distribution whose mean is equal to the autarky deterministic price ratio are direct consequences of their assumption that production decisions are not in line with consumption preferences [see also Kemp and Ohyama (1978) on this point]. It is easy to see that in the case in which production decisions are consistent with consumption preferences, the first-best policy consists of no government intervention.

Moreover, even if one accepts their model, it is hard to see how their suggested policy measures will bring about the optimal allocation. Clearly, if the mean of the foreign price distribution is equal to the autarky price ratio, then price stabilization at the mean will prevent foreign trade, and this is a feasible policy. However, if the mean foreign price is not equal to the autarky price ratio, then there is no guarantee that the expected deficit in the government budget will equal zero (Hanoch, 1974). If the expected deficit is positive, this policy is not feasible. If the expected deficit is negative, then it is not optimal to stabilize the price at the mean. In any case, Hanoch (1974) showed that stabilization of a price with a balanced budget on average (so that the expected deficit of the stabilizing authority is zero) is always welfare-reducing in a case such as the one considered here.

Contrary to the Batra–Russell claim, a consumption subsidy for the import good is not the optimal policy in their model. Optimality requires a shift only of the production point; one can leave export decisions to the private sector. This can be accomplished by a producer subsidy for the export good.

Finally, let us comment on the class of models represented by (4.1). Observe that by deciding ex ante on the level of exports of the first commodity, x, the level of imports of the second commodity, $x/p(\alpha)$, is random. This makes the consumption of the first commodity deter-

---

[1] Brainard and Cooper (1968) also advocate government intervention, but in the form of protection. However, their formal analysis does not provide justification for such policies.

ministic and the consumption of the second commodity random. There is no natural justification for the ex-ante determination of exports. For example, it may happen that an ex-ante determination of imports, making exports random, will provide a higher level of expected utility. Moreover, a simultaneous ex-ante determination of autonomous exports and imports, such as in Ruffin (1974a), provides an even higher expected utility level (see below).

In all of the models discussed so far, there is nothing that guarantees that a country which is opened to international trade will be actively engaged in such trade. As in the usual deterministic trade models, there exist limiting cases in which trade will not take place. However, Ruffin (1974a) showed that in a world in which there exist both autonomous exports and autonomous imports, a country will always actively engage in international trade, regardless of foreign price distributions; he called it the nonautarky theorem.

Ruffin's model can be presented as follows. By assuming, as he did, that output levels are fixed, the choice problem is

(4.2)   choose x_1 and x_2

                to maximize

$$Eu\left[Q_1 - x_1 + p(\alpha)x_2, Q_2 - x_2 + \frac{x_1}{p(\alpha)}\right]$$

where x_j is the autonomous export of good j, $x_j \gtrless 0$.

It is clear from (4.2) that this model is less constrained than the previously discussed models, since (4.2) reduces to (4.1) (apart from the production decisions) if we add the constraint $x_2 = 0$. In this framework, Ruffin (1974a) shows that $x_1 = x_2 = 0$ is never an optimal solution, provided the price distribution is nondegenerate. Observe, however, that if $p(\alpha)$ obtains a given value with probability one, that is, $p(\alpha)$ is state independent, the nonautarky theorem does not hold for all price values.

The nonautarky theorem can be proved as follows. Suppose we choose $x_1 = \varepsilon a_1$ and $x_2 = \varepsilon a_2$. If for ε sufficiently small we can find a_1 and a_2 such that this is preferred to $x_1 = x_2 = 0$, then autarky is obviously not the solution of (4.2). Define

$$\phi(\varepsilon) \equiv Eu\left[Q_1 - \varepsilon a_1 + p(\alpha)\varepsilon a_2, Q_2 - \varepsilon a_2 + \frac{\varepsilon a_1}{p(\alpha)}\right]$$

Then, the derivative of $\phi(\cdot)$ with respect to ε, evaluated at $\varepsilon = 0$, is

(4.3) $\phi'(0) = u_1(Q_1, Q_2)\left\{a_2[Ep(\alpha) - \text{MRS}]\right.$

$$+ a_1\left[\text{MRS} - \frac{1}{E[1/p(\alpha)]}\right]E\frac{1}{p(\alpha)}\right\}$$

where $\text{MRS} = u_2(Q_1, Q_2)/u_1(Q_1, Q_2)$ is the autarky marginal rate of substitution in consumption.

If the distribution of p is not degenerate, then

$$E\frac{1}{p(\alpha)} > \frac{1}{Ep(\alpha)}$$

because $1/p$ is a strictly convex function of p. Hence, it is impossible to have both brackets in (4.3) equal to zero. This means that a_1 and a_2 can always be chosen so as to make $\phi'(0) > 0$, which implies that some trade is always desirable.

All of the foregoing models share a common undesirable feature: They do not have a general equilibrium representation. This important fact is explained in the remainder of this section.

Generally speaking, price uncertainty has to be induced by more basic random elements, since prices are endogenous to the world economy. Uncertain preferences, uncertain initial endowments, and uncertain technology may induce price uncertainty, since each may cause the market clearing conditions to be state dependent.

Suppose that we introduce these elements into the models considered in this section, and we extend the models to a many-country world. Then, it can be shown (as we shall do) that in this case the world market clearing conditions are state independent. This means that the endogenous market clearing prices are also state independent, which implies that the institutional framework employed in these models—that is, ex-ante trading decisions without recontracting in spot markets after a realization of a state of the world—prevents the usual basic causes of price uncertainty from inducing price uncertainty.

In order to demonstrate this point, consider a two-country world in which each country is a Ruffin-type country. Denote country j by a superscript j, $j = 1, 2$. Assume that Q_1^j and Q_2^j are random initial endowments of country j; that there exist only two states of the world, $\alpha = 1$ and $\alpha = 2$; and that $\pi^j(\alpha)$, $\alpha = 1, 2$, are the subjective probabilities of country j. We denote by $y(\alpha)$ the value of variable y in state α. Now, country j solves the problem

(4.4)   choose x_1^j and x_2^j

to maximize

$$\pi^j(1)u^j\left[Q_1^j(1) - x_1^j + p(1)x_2^j, Q_2^j(1) - x_2^j + \frac{x_1^j}{p(1)}\right]$$

$$+ \pi^j(2)u^j\left[Q_1^j(2) - x_1^j + p(2)x_2^j, Q_2^j(2) - x_2^j + \frac{x_1^j}{p(2)}\right]$$

The solution depends, of course, on all of the exogenous variables and on prices. Let us express only the dependence of the optimal x_i^j's on prices—$x_i^j = x_i^j[p(1), p(2)]$, $i = 1, 2, j = 1, 2$—since prices are endogenous to the world, despite the fact that they are exogenous to each country separately.

The equilibrium prices are determined so as to clear both markets for goods 1 and 2 in each state of the world. Because of Walras' law, it is sufficient to assure clearing of the market for good 1 in each state of the world. Suppose that $p(1)$ and $p(2)$ are indeed equilibrium prices; then they must satisfy

(4.5) $$\sum_{j=1}^{2} \{Q_1^j(\alpha) - x_1^j[p(1), p(2)] + p(\alpha)x_2^j[p(1), p(2)]\}$$

$$= \sum_{j=1}^{2} Q_1^j(\alpha), \qquad \alpha = 1, 2$$

From (4.5), we obtain

(4.6) $$p(\alpha) = \frac{\sum_{j=1}^{2} x_1^j[p(1), p(2)]}{\sum_{j=1}^{2} x_2^j[p(1), p(2)]}, \qquad \alpha = 1, 2$$

Since the right-hand side of (4.6) is state independent, $p(1) = p(2)$; that is, p is also state independent.[2]

It is clear from the preceding argument that the ex-ante trading models are valid only for a single country, provided there are other countries which engage in ex-post trading decisions. However, if it is possible to make trading decisions ex post (that is, when prices are already known), it pays to never make such decisions ex ante (that is, before prices are known).

---

[2] One may argue that the distribution of p is subjective. However, if the *actual p* does not vary across states of the world, it is inconceivable that individuals will expect it to vary. This is particularly true if one considers these models as long-run models.

The economic interpretation of state-independent prices is that we have, in fact, future markets. In this case, Ruffin's model is identical to the other models discussed in this section, since in this case $x_1 - px_2$ can be considered as the single decision variable x. But this model can be further enriched by adding ex-post spot markets—markets which enable trade after the realization of a state of the world. If this is done, ex-ante prices on future markets are known with certainty, whereas spot-market prices are random.

4.3 EX-POST COMMODITY TRADING DECISIONS

The models which employ ex-post commodity trading decisions embody a two-stage decision-making process. In the first stage, before the resolution of uncertainty, each country determines the allocation of its factors of production. In the second stage, after the resolution of uncertainty, each country makes its consumption decisions using foreign trade. Uncertainty may originate from technological factors, from prices, or from preferences.

Let us start the discussion with Ricardian-type models. These were developed by Kemp and Liviatan (1973), Ruffin (1974b), and Turnovsky (1974), and their general form can be represented as follows.

Let $l_j\,(=1/a_{Lj})$ be the output–labor ratio in sector j, and let p be the relative price of good 2. The relative price and the output–input ratios may be random variables. Let L_j be the labor input allocated to sector j, and L the total labor endowment of the home country (L is not random).

Suppose, for the moment, that the labor allocation (L_1, L_2) has been chosen. When the state of the world α realizes, the relative price $p(\alpha)$ and outputs $l_1(\alpha)L_1$ and $l_2(\alpha)L_2$ become known. The country then solves the usual consumption and trading-decision problem:[3]

(4.7)   choose $c_1, c_2 \geq 0$

to maximize

$u(c_1, c_2)$

subject to

$c_1 + p(\alpha)c_2 \leq l_1(\alpha)L_1 + p(\alpha)l_2(\alpha)L_2$

---

[3] One can also make the utility function $u(\cdot)$ depend on the state of the world α. This can be interpreted as random preferences, or—as Kemp and Liviatan (1973) prefer—as the existence of a nontradeable good whose supply is random. We do not introduce this complication because it is unnecessary for our discussion.

The solution to this problem yields ordinary demand functions $c_j[p(\alpha), l_1(\alpha)L_1 + p(\alpha)l_2(\alpha)L_2], j = 1, 2$. Substituting these demand functions into the utility function $u(\cdot)$, we obtain the indirect utility function $v(\cdot)$ which is defined by

$$(4.8) \qquad v[p(\alpha), l_1(\alpha)L_1 + p(\alpha)l_2(\alpha)L_2]$$
$$\equiv u\{c_1[p(\alpha), l_1(\alpha)L_1 + p(\alpha)l_2(\alpha)L_2],$$
$$c_2[p(\alpha), l_1(\alpha)L_1 + p(\alpha)l_2(\alpha)L_2]\}$$

Now, turning to input decisions, the country chooses L_1 and L_2 so as to maximize the expected value of the indirect utility function:

$$(4.9) \qquad \text{choose} \quad L_1, L_2 \geq 0$$
$$\text{to maximize}$$
$$Ev[p(\alpha), l_1(\alpha)L_1 + p(\alpha)l_2(\alpha)L_2]$$
$$\text{subject to}$$
$$L_1 + L_2 \leq L$$

Assuming that the utility function $u(\cdot)$ exhibits risk aversion (that is, it is strictly concave), the combinations of L_1 and L_2 which keep the expected utility level constant at a fixed level can be represented by a convex-to-the-origin indifference curve, provided the distributions of at least one of the pair $l_1(\alpha)$ and $p(\alpha)l_2(\alpha)$ are nondegenerate and they are not perfectly correlated. If these distributions are degenerate— that is, if $l_1(\alpha)$ and $p(\alpha)l_2(\alpha)$ obtain fixed values with probability one—or if they are perfectly correlated, the indifference curves are straight lines. A graphic solution to problem (4.9) is presented in Figure 4.1.

UU represents the highest achievable expected utility level for a country endowed with L units of labor. Generally speaking, this country will not specialize completely in production, contrary to the deterministic case. Ruffin (1974b) and Turnovsky (1974) provide conditions which assure complete specialization. In the deterministic case, the indifference curves are straight lines and specialization is the rule.

Observe that the indifference curves between L_1 and L_2 depend, apart from preferences, on the distributions of the technological parameters and prices. Changes in these distributions twist the indifference curves. From this, one can see that by an appropriate choice of these distributions, one can make the country specialize in either good 1 or good 2. Assuming fixed output–labor ratios, Kemp and Liviatan (1973) and Turnovsky (1974) showed that a country may specialize in the production of the good in which it has a comparative

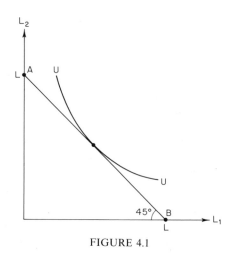

FIGURE 4.1

disadvantage (that is, the good whose relative output–input ratio is the lowest). An example of this type is provided in Chapter 7.

This result stems from the fact that the traditional definition of comparative advantage does not take into account elements of risk. If, for example, the country has a comparative advantage in the second commodity and the relative price of this commodity is random, then insurance considerations may dictate diversification in production. If, in addition, the preferences of the country are biased toward the first commodity, then insurance considerations may even dictate specialization in the first commodity.

Generally speaking, the allocation of labor in this case also depends on risk preferences and preferences over commodities. There is no independence of production decisions from preferences, as in the deterministic case. If there is sufficient risk aversion, one would expect incomplete specialization to be the optimal policy—provided, of course, that the marginal (average) rate of transformation in production lies within some "reasonable" limits of the support of the price distribution.

We conclude this discussion with an example that demonstrates incomplete specialization in this type of a model.

EXAMPLE 4.1   Suppose that $u(\cdot)$ is a Cobb–Douglas utility function:

$$u(c_1, c_2) = [\gamma c_1^{(1-\beta)} c_2^{\beta}]^{\mu},$$
$$0 < \beta < 1, \quad 0 < \mu < 1, \quad \gamma > 0$$

Since $\mu < 1$, the utility function exhibits risk aversion, and the degree of risk aversion increases as μ decreases.

By an appropriate choice of the constant γ, the indirect utility function which is defined in (4.8) becomes (we omit the alphas)

$$v(p, l_1 L_1 + pl_2 L_2) \equiv p^{-\beta\mu}(l_1 L_1 + pl_2 L_2)^{\mu}$$

Assume that the output–labor ratios are nonrandom; only the price ratio $p = p_2/p_1$ is random. Then, the maximal expected utility level achievable for a labor allocation (L_1, L_2) is

$$U(L_1, L_2) \equiv Ep(\alpha)^{-\beta\mu}[l_1 L_1 + p(\alpha)l_2 L_2]^{\mu}$$

The indifference curve in Figure 4.1 represents combinations of L_1 and L_2 which keep $U(L_1, L_2)$ constant. The marginal rate of substitution between L_1 and L_2 along such an indifference curve is given by

$$\mathrm{MRS}(L_1, L_2) \equiv \frac{\partial U}{\partial L_1}(L_1, L_2) \bigg/ \frac{\partial U}{\partial L_2}(L_1, L_2)$$

$$= \frac{l_1}{l_2} \frac{Ep(\alpha)^{-\beta\mu}[l_1 L_1 + p(\alpha)l_2 L_2]^{\mu-1}}{Ep(\alpha)^{1-\beta\mu}[l_1 L_1 + p(\alpha)l_2 L_2]^{\mu-1}}$$

This implies that at the corner points A and B in Figure 4.1 the marginal rates of substitution are

$$\mathrm{MRS}(0, L) = \frac{l_1 Ep(\alpha)^{\mu(1-\beta)-1}}{l_2 Ep(\alpha)^{\mu(1-\beta)}}$$

and

$$\mathrm{MRS}(L, 0) = \frac{l_1 Ep(\alpha)^{-\beta\mu}}{l_2 Ep(\alpha)^{1-\beta\mu}}$$

respectively. Clearly, if $\mathrm{MRS}(L, 0) < 1 < \mathrm{MRS}(0, L)$—that is, if at point A the slope of the indifference curve is larger than one, and at point B the slope of the indifference curve is smaller than one—then the country will choose not to specialize in production. Now, since

$$\lim_{\mu \to 0} \mathrm{MRS}(0, L) = \frac{l_1}{l_2} E \frac{1}{p(\alpha)}$$

and

$$\lim_{\mu \to 0} \mathrm{MRS}(L, 0) = \frac{l_1}{l_2} \frac{1}{Ep(\alpha)}$$

and since $E[1/p(\alpha)] > [1/Ep(\alpha)]$ if the distribution of p is nondegenerate, then if

$$E\frac{1}{p(\alpha)} > \frac{l_2}{l_1} > \frac{1}{Ep(\alpha)}$$

the country will not specialize in production if it is sufficiently risk averse. Hence, if the expected value of the relative price of commodity 1, $E[1/p(\alpha)]$, is larger than its relative cost ratio l_2/l_1, and the expected relative price of commodity 2, $Ep(\alpha)$, is also larger than its relative cost ratio l_1/l_2, then a sufficiently risk averse country will always choose not to specialize in production.

Anderson and Riley (1976) analyzed the impact of uncertainty on the choice of production and the level of welfare of a small country that faces random foreign prices. Using the definition of the indirect utility function from (4.8), their choice problem can be represented as

(4.10)   choose $Q_2 \geq 0$

                         to maximize

                         $Ev[p(\alpha), F(Q_2) + p(\alpha)Q_2]$

where $F(\cdot)$ represents the transformation curve, and $Q_1 = F(Q_2)$.

The first-order condition for an interior solution is

(4.11) $MRT(Q_2{}^*) \equiv -F'(Q_2{}^*)$

$$= \frac{Ep(\alpha)v_1[p(\alpha), F(Q_2{}^*) + p(\alpha)Q_2{}^*]}{Ev_1[p(\alpha), F(Q_2{}^*) + p(\alpha)Q_2{}^*]}$$

where $-F'(\cdot)$ is the marginal rate of transformation in production (MRT), and $v_1(\cdot)$ is the marginal utility of income. Thus, the country equates its marginal rate of transformation in production with a *weighted* average of the relative price, where the marginal utilities of income multiplied by the respective probabilities are used as weights. To see this, rewrite the right-hand side of (4.11), using $\pi(\alpha)$ to denote the probability of state α, to obtain

$$\sum_{\alpha=1}^{S} p(\alpha) \left[\frac{\pi(\alpha)v_1(\alpha)}{\sum_{\alpha'=1}^{S} \pi(\alpha')v_1(\alpha')} \right]$$

Anderson and Riley (1976) start by comparing the allocation of production that obtains from (4.11) with the allocation of production that obtains when the country faces a certain price ratio which is equal to the expected value of p. Using (4.11), we obtain

$$(4.12) \quad \text{MRT}(Q_2{}^*) - Ep(\alpha) = \frac{1}{Ev_1[p(\alpha), F(Q_2{}^*) + p(\alpha)Q_2{}^*]}$$
$$\times \text{Cov}\{p(\alpha), v_1[p(\alpha), F(Q_2{}^*) + p(\alpha)Q_2{}^*]\}$$

Since in case of certainty the country will choose to produce $\bar{Q}_2$ at which the MRT equals the relative price, (4.12) implies that it will choose to produce $\bar{Q}_2 > Q_2{}^*$ if the covariance between p and the marginal utility of income is negative, and it will choose $\bar{Q}_2 < Q_2{}^*$ if this covariance is positive. Hence, if $v_1(\cdot)$ increases (decreases) in p on the support of the distribution of p, $\bar{Q}_2 < Q_2{}^* \ (\bar{Q}_2 > Q_2{}^*)$.

Differentiating $v_1(\cdot)$ with respect to p, and using the preceding monotonicity results, they conclude that

(a)   if risk aversion is sufficiently low, $\bar{Q}_2 > Q_2{}^*$, and
(b)   if risk aversion is sufficiently high, then $\bar{Q}_2 > Q_2{}^*$ if commodity 2 is exported at all relevant price ratios, and $\bar{Q}_2 < Q_2{}^*$ if commodity 1 is exported at all relevant price ratios.

This implies that sufficiently high-risk aversion assures less specialization in the case of fluctuating prices.

Anderson and Riley (1976) also show that mean-preserving spreads of the price distribution have an ambiguous impact on the choice of production as well as on the level of welfare as measured by the level of the expected utility. However, *small* mean-preserving spreads around the *autarky* relative price have welfare-improving effects. To this we wish to add the simple observation that *any* price distribution is preferable to autarky (and hence to a nonrandom price ratio which equals the autarky price ratio), because this assures—by the standard gains from trade argument—a higher welfare level in *every* state of the world, which means a higher expected utility level. We will return to this point in Chapter 9.

Batra (1975) analyzed a Heckscher–Ohlin type model with technological uncertainty. He assumed that the output of the first industry depends on the value of a random multiplicative element, while the output of the second industry is nonrandom; and that input decisions of an industry are based on maximization of an expected risk averse utility function of profits. This model is consistent only with the interpretation that each sector is owned by a *different* group of individuals. The group that owns the first industry bears the entire risk of that industry, since there are no financial markets to enable risk sharing with other individuals in the economy.

The problem of the first industry is

(4.13)   choose $L_1, K_1 \geq 0$

to maximize

$$EU_1[p_1\theta_1(\alpha)f_1(L_1, K_1) - wL_1 - rK_1]$$

where L_1 is the labor input in sector 1, K_1 the capital input in sector 1, U_1 the utility function of profits in sector 1, p_1 the price of good 1, θ_1 the random production parameter which obtains different values in different states of the world, w the wage rate, and r the rental rate on capital. Since there is no uncertainty in the second sector, its input decisions are made so as to maximize profits.

From (4.13), we obtain the first-order conditions

(4.14a) $$RM_1 p_1 \frac{\partial f_1}{\partial L_1} = w$$

(4.14b) $$RM_1 p_2 \frac{\partial f_1}{\partial K_1} = r$$

where

(4.15) $$RM_1 = \frac{EU_1'(\alpha)\theta_1(\alpha)}{EU_1'(\alpha)}$$

is, in the terminology of Sandmo (1971), the risk margin of sector 1. Hence, the value of marginal product, which is equated to the factor price, includes a risk margin (or, perhaps, a risk premium).

The risk margin depends on *absolute* levels of factor inputs—and these in turn depend in equilibrium on, among other things, the factor endowments of the economy. Hence, in this case the relationship between commodity and factor prices also depends on total factor endowments. This means that the standard theorems such as factor price equalization, Stolper–Samuelson, and Rybczynski need not hold. However, assuming that $U_1(\cdot)$ exhibits decreasing absolute risk aversion, Batra (1975) showed that the Stolper–Samuelson theorem holds in his framework.[4] The factor price equalization theorem cannot be saved

---

[4] Batra claimed that decreasing absolute risk aversion is also sufficient for the Rybczynski theorem to hold. However, this was disproved by Das (1977). In Chapter 7, in the context of our model we shall provide an example with decreasing absolute risk aversion in which the Stolper–Samuelson theorem does not hold.

because, as we mentioned previously, the relationship between commodity and factor prices also depends on factor endowments.

Mayer (1976) argued that Batra's model is an intermediate-run rather than a long-run model. The reason for this argument is as follows. In the long run, the expected utility of profits of a single firm has to be equal in both sectors, and it has to be equal to the utility of zero profits. For if the expected utility of profits in an industry exceeds the utility of zero profits, then new firms will enter the industry and they will drive down the expected utility of profits in this industry. If, on the other hand, the expected utility of profits in an industry falls short of the utility of zero profits, then firms will leave the industry, thus driving up the expected utility of profits of the remaining firms. Batra did not impose this condition. Therefore, his model can be interpreted as an intermediate-run model in which the number of firms is *fixed* in every industry.

In order to analyze the long-run case, Mayer (1976) employs a Heckscher–Ohlin model in which there is only price uncertainty. Firms are assumed to maximize the expected utility of profits, which implies that for each output level, a firm minimizes the cost of production. Hence, assuming constant returns to scale, the labor and capital output ratios employed by a firm in industry j—a_{Lj} and a_{Kj}, respectively— depend only on factor prices $a_{Lj}(w, r)$ and $a_{Kj}(w, r)$.

In a given industry j, all firms are assumed to be identical. Therefore, a typical firm in industry j chooses its output level Q_j so as to solve

(4.16)   choose $Q_j \geq 0$

to maximize

$$EU_j\{Q_j[p_j(\alpha) - a_{Lj}(w, r)w - a_{Kj}(w, r)r]\}$$
$$j = 1, 2$$

The long-run equilibrium condition for a representative firm in sector j is

(4.17) $EU_j\{Q_j[p_j(\alpha) - a_{Lj}(w, r)w - a_{Kj}(w, r)r]\} = a$
$$j = 1, 2$$

where a is the expected utility of zero profits.

Apart from (4.16) and (4.17), there are also the full-employment conditions

(4.18) $a_{L1}(w, r)Q_1{}^* + a_{L2}(w, r)Q_2{}^* = L$

(4.19) $a_{K1}(w, r)Q_1{}^* + a_{K2}(w, r)Q_2{}^* = K$

where Q_j^* is the output of *sector j*. The number of firms in industry j is given by Q_j^*/Q_j.

Now, the first-order conditions from (4.16), together with (4.17), provide four equations in four unknowns. The unknowns are Q_1, Q_2, w, and r. Hence, factor prices are independent of factor endowments. This, and the factor market clearing conditions (4.18) and (4.19), imply immediately that the Rybczynski theorem is valid. Moreover, for a given distribution of commodity prices, a change in the output of an industry is achieved by means of a change in the number of firms in the industry; the optimal output level for a single firm is not affected by changes in factor endowments (so long as there is incomplete specialization).

Mayer also shows that the Stolper–Samuelson theorem is valid when changes in commodity prices are replaced by changes in the expected value of commodity prices, keeping all higher moments of the price distribution constant.

It is also clear from (4.16) and (4.17) that if two countries have (in addition to the same technologies) the same utility functions over profits and the same probability assessments, then if they face the same commodity price distribution they will have the same factor prices and the same firm size in each industry. In this case we have a factor price equalization theorem.

4.4 FINANCIAL MARKETS

The papers surveyed in previous sections did not consider markets for risk sharing. Kemp and Liviatan (1973) are an exception. They considered contingent commodity markets of the Arrow–Debreu type. In this framework, countries specialize according to comparative advantage. The reason for this result is that in the presence of these markets the value of a random return is market determined and equal to all market participants. Hence, there is an objective valuation of each output distribution and specialization takes place according to comparative costs.

A recent contribution by Pomery (1976) also discusses Arrow–Debreu contingent markets. For the one-commodity, two-state, and two-country case, he provided a detailed characterization of the pattern of trade and the market determination of the risk premium. He showed how differences in probability assessments as well as attitudes toward risk generate incentives for trading in contingent claims. The nature of these results can be described as follows.

Consider the home country which has an endowment of $e(\alpha)$ units of the single good in state α, $\alpha = 1, 2$. The country solves

(4.20)   choose $c(1), c(2) \geq 0$

to maximize

$$W[c(1), c(2)] \equiv \pi(1)u[c(1)] + \pi(2)u[c(2)]$$

subject to

$$c(1) + gc(2) \leq e(1) + ge(2)$$

where $g \equiv g(2)/g(1)$ is the relative price of state-2 contingent goods, and $\pi(\alpha)$ is the subjective probability assessment of state α.

The marginal rate of substitution between state-2 and state-1 consumption is given by

$$(4.21) \qquad MRS^W[c(1), c(2)] \equiv \frac{\pi(2)u'[c(2)]}{\pi(1)u'[c(1)]}$$

The solution to (4.20) occurs at a point at which g equals MRS^W on the budget line. This is a standard result in consumer theory, and we can represent the present solution by means of indifference curves and budget lines. Here, however, preferences (indifference curves) between $c(1)$ and $c(2)$ depend on two things: (a) probability beliefs, and (b) attitudes toward risk, since whenever $c(2) \neq c(1)$ the ratio $u'[c(2)]/u'[c(1)]$ depends on the degree of concavity of $u(\cdot)$.

Prior to international trade in contingent claims, the equilibrium relative price in the economy of state-2 consumption is

$$(4.22) \qquad \hat{g} \equiv \frac{\pi(2)u'[e(2)]}{\pi(1)u'[e(1)]}$$

This equilibrium is presented graphically in Figure 4.2. Point E is the endowment point as well as equilibrium consumption prior to international trade. The indifference curve of $W(\cdot)$ that passes through E defines the pretrade equilibrium relative price $\hat{g}$ by its slope at E, given by line BB.

Observe that the slope of *every* indifference curve at its intersection with the 45° ray through the origin is just equal to the probability ratio $\pi(2)/\pi(1)$, irrespective of attitudes toward risk. This is so, since at

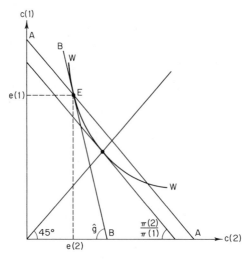

FIGURE 4.2

actuarially fair prices, that is, prices which are proportional to probabilities, risk-averse individuals contract so as to eliminate all risks, thus assure themselves of a certain (state-independent) level of consumption. But this means that state-2 contingent goods, where state 2 is relatively poorly endowed, will sell at a premium while state-1 contingent goods will sell at a discount, compared to actuarially fair prices.

Now suppose there is also a foreign country which is similar to the country already described; we denote its variables by asterisks. Let $\hat{g}^*$ be the pretrade equilibrium relative price in the foreign country of state-2 contingent goods. Then, clearly, when international trade in contingent commodities opens, the home country will export state-2 contingent goods if $\hat{g} < \hat{g}^*$ and it will export state-1 contingent goods if $\hat{g} > \hat{g}^*$, where

(4.23) $$\hat{g}^* \equiv \frac{\pi^*(2)u^{*\prime}[e^*(2)]}{\pi^*(1)u^{*\prime}[e^*(1)]}$$

If both economies have the same endowment and attitudes toward risk, there will be trade if and only if they have different probability beliefs. By comparing (4.23) with (4.22), it is easy to see that in this case the country with the lower probability assessment of state α will export state-α contingent goods and it will import contingent goods in the other state.

Suppose that both countries have the same endowment and the same probability beliefs but different attitudes toward risk. For concreteness, let the foreign country be globally more risk averse than the home country; that is, u^* is an increasing strictly concave transformation of u. Then, by comparing (4.23) with (4.22), it is easy to see that $\hat{g} < \hat{g}^*$ when $e(1) > e(2)$. Hence, the more risk-averse country will export state-α contingent goods, where α is the relatively well-endowed state. In this case the expected consumption level of the more risk-averse country will decline as a result of trade, while the expected consumption level of the less risk-averse country will increase. This can be verified by means of Figure 4.2, by observing that the consumption point of the home country will be above AA if it is to export state-2 contingent goods, which has to be the case since $e(1) > e(2)$ in that figure. In this case we may say that the more risk-averse country is paying a premium to the less risk-averse country.

In another part of his dissertation, Pomery discussed trade in shares of random endowments. This is a case of incomplete markets which comes close to the approach that we developed (Helpman and Razin, 1975), and which is the basis for the present study. Pomery recognized the importance of the interactions between ex-post trade in commodities and ex-ante trade in endowment shares, but he stopped short of analyzing their implications. The interactions between ex-post trading in goods and ex-ante trading in firm-ownership shares, and their implications for resource allocation, are the central theme of the present investigation.

REFERENCES

Anderson, J., and Riley, J. G. (1976). International trade with fluctuating prices, *International Economic Review* **17**, 76–97.

Bardhan, P. K. (1971). Uncertainty, resource allocation and factor shares in a two-sector model, MIT Working Paper No. 79.

Batra, R. N. (1975). Production uncertainty and the Heckscher–Ohlin theorem, *Review of Economic Studies* **42**, 259–268.

Batra, R. N., and Russell, W. R. (1974). Gains from trade under uncertainty, *American Economic Review* **64**, 1040–1048.

Brainard, W. C., and Cooper, R. N. (1968). Uncertainty and diversification of international trade, *Food Research Institute Studies in Agricultural Economics, Trade and Development* **8**, 257–285.

Das, S. K. (1977). Uncertainty and the Heckscher–Ohlin theorem: A comment, *Review of Economic Studies* **44**, 189–190.

Hanoch, G. (1974). Desirability of price stabilization or destabilization, HIER Discussion Paper No. 351.

Helpman, E., and Razin, A. (1975). Uncertainty and international trade in the presence of stock markets, Working Paper No. 96, The Foerder Institute for Economic Research, Tel-Aviv Univ. (October).

Kemp, M. C., and Liviatan, N. (1973). Production and trade patterns under uncertainty, *Economic Record* **49**, 215–227.

Kemp, M. C., and Ohyama, M. (1978). The gain from free trade under conditions of uncertainty, *Journal of International Economics* **8**, 139–141.

Mayer, W. (1976). The Rybczynski, Stolper–Samuelson, and factor price equalization theorems under price uncertainty, *American Economic Review* **66**, 796–808.

Pomery, J. G. (1976). International trade and uncertainty: Simple general equilibrium models involving randomness, Unpublished Ph.D. Dissertation, Department of Economics, Univ. of Rochester.

Ruffin, R. J. (1974a). International trade under uncertainty, *Journal of International Economics* **4**, 243–260.

Ruffin, R. J. (1974b). Comparative advantage under uncertainty, *Journal of International Economics* **4**, 261–274.

Sandmo, A. (1971). On the theory of the competitive firm under price uncertainty, *American Economic Review* **61**, 65–73.

Turnovsky, S. J. (1974). Technological and price uncertainty in a Ricardian model of international trade, *Review of Economic Studies* **41**, 201–217.

Chapter 5

A Stock Market Economy

Uncertainty elements appear in various branches of economics, and they play a central role in some. For example, the theory of finance and the theory of insurance are concerned primarily with trade in "risks." The existence of risks which must be borne by economic agents provides an incentive to develop markets for beneficial risk sharing. Arrow (1963–1964) showed, for example, that if there exist markets for elementary securities in all states of the world, where an elementary security provides a return of one dollar in a particular state of the world and zero in all other states, then—provided price expectations are correct—the resulting allocation will be Pareto efficient. In this world, firms can maintain profit maximization as their objective, since they can use elementary security prices to evaluate distributions of profits, or they can *sell* their profits in the different states of the world on markets for elementary securities.

In practice, there are no markets for elementary securities, nor are there sufficient securities of other types to generate complete markets. In the Western industrial world, stock, bond, and future markets provide the main arena for risk-sharing arrangements. Security trading is a widespread phenomenon both within countries and across countries.

The literature surveyed in the previous chapter had little to say about the role of securities. It is, however, natural to consider international trade under uncertainty in a world with security markets. This does not mean that all securities have to be traded internationally; we may have nontraded securities, just as we have nontraded goods. However, one'would expect the introduction of security markets to have significant effects on the theory of international trade. It permits the analysis of a considerably wider range of problems than those considered by earlier writers—in particular, problems which stem from the interaction of trade in goods and securities. To proceed in this direction, we have to integrate the theory of financial markets into the theory of international trade. Consequently, this chapter describes an economy with a stock market.

Our presentation rests heavily on the pioneering paper by Diamond (1967) and on the presentation of Diamond's model by Hart (1974). We will put the stock market model into a framework which fits the standard Ricardian and Heckscher–Ohlin models of international trade, so that by removing the uncertainty elements one will obtain the standard trade models.

In order to keep things as clear as possible, the exposition uses a two-sector one-consumer economy, and we discuss only the small-country case. An extension to a world of many countries, many commodities, and many factors of production is straightforward.[1] In the next chapter, we discuss the implications of the existence of a safe bond; here, we assume that equities are the only available securities.

5.1   THE FRAMEWORK

Our economy consists of firms and consumers who operate in an uncertain environment generated by random production technology or random world prices. These random elements produce an incentive to develop financial capital markets, whose existence—in the form of stock markets—we assume. Domestic financial capital markets may or may not be integrated into world capital markets. If domestic capital

---

[1] The stock market model generates difficulties in the presence of more than one good; the existence of many factors of production poses no problem (Diamond, 1967; Hart, 1974, 1975). We overcome these difficulties by assuming a unique equilibrium. This assumption may not be strong in a two-commodity world, but it is strong in a many-commodity world.

markets are not integrated into world capital markets (that is, there is no international trade in securities), they enable risk-sharing only among domestic residents. However, if domestic capital markets are integrated into world capital markets, they permit international risk-sharing. Since we deal with international trade, we assume that there is international trade in commodities.

Input decisions have to be made before the resolution of uncertainty. As a result, firms face random profits and cannot undertake profit maximization. Instead, we assume—following Diamond (1967)—that firms choose their input levels so as to maximize their net value on the stock market; this procedure is equivalent to profit maximization whenever the relevant random elements become degenerate (that is, their value becomes known with certainty). After the resolution of uncertainty, returns are realized and the firms distribute them to their final stockholders.

Individuals play a double role in this economy. In the first stage—before the resolution of uncertainty—individuals choose (among other things) a portfolio by means of trading in the stock market. An equity in a firm entitles the stockholder to a share in the random return of the firm. This share equals the inverse of the number of outstanding equities of the firm. This is the stage in which individuals play the role of investors.

In the second stage—after the resolution of uncertainty—individuals use the proceeds from portfolios to purchase commodities. This is the stage in which they play the role of consumers.[2]

Clearly, the two roles are interrelated. The ultimate goal of a portfolio chosen in the first stage is to provide consumption in the second stage. Hence, portfolio choice depends on preferences over consumption goods—but it also depends on probability beliefs, price expectations, and attitudes toward risk.

5.2 FIRMS

Consider a two-sector economy which produces two commodities, good 1 and good 2, by means of only labor or capital *and* labor. Each sector is composed of identical firms, and the output of each firm depends on its employment of capital and labor and on the state of

---

[2] In Chapter 11 we consider a dynamic version of a stock market economy in which individuals consume and trade in securities simultaneously in every period.

nature that realizes. In particular, in every state of nature α, $\alpha = 1, 2, \ldots, S$, the output of firm j is

(5.1) $Q_j(\alpha) = \theta_j(\alpha) f_j(L_j, K_j)$ for $\alpha = 1, 2, \ldots, S$

where θ_j is a positive-valued random variable, $f_j(\cdot)$ a standard neo-classical linear homogeneous production function, or a Ricardian-type production function [in the Ricardian case, $f_j(L_j, K_j) = l_j L_j$], L_j the labor input in firm j, K_j the capital input in firm j, and Q_j the output of firm j, which is also random. Since all firms in a given sector are identical and $f_j(\cdot)$ is linear homogeneous, (5.1) also describes the output of the sector to which firm j belongs if L_j and K_j are interpreted as the total factor inputs in this sector. We use this aggregation procedure, and from now on we use sectors as the production units. The index j is used to denote sectors; $j = 1, 2$.

Our technological specification has two important features. First, the input decisions—which are not state-dependent—have to be made *before* a state of nature realizes. This resembles an agricultural process in which the land is cultivated before it is known how many inches of rain will fall. Second, the uncertainty is of the multiplicative type; that is, an increase in inputs increases output in every state of nature by the same factor of proportionality. This feature permits a simple characterization of the behavior of each sector if we are willing to assume—as indeed we are—that firms maximize their net value. By net value we mean the value of the firm to its *initial* stockholders.[3]

We assume that no bonds exist. In this case there are two ways in which a firm can finance its input costs (assuming that it has no resources initially): it can pass these costs directly to its initial owners, or it can float new equities. In either case, the initial stockholders bear all *factor* costs. In the first case they pay all factor costs, and the value of their equity is the entire stock market value of the firm; in the second case they bear no direct costs, but the value of their equity is the market

---

[3] The assumption of multiplicative production uncertainty is maintained through the entire study, because there is no good general equilibrium theory of financial markets for nonmultiplicative uncertainties. On the difficulties involved in modeling nonmultiplicative uncertainties in a general equilibrium framework, see Diamond (1967) and Helpman and Razin (1978). It can be shown that in the case of multiplicative uncertainty, net value maximization is in the best interest of the firm stockholders independent of their preferences and attitudes toward risk. In the absence of multiplicative uncertainty there will be no conflict among the stockholders if a condition called the "spanning condition" is satisfied (Ekern and Wilson, 1974). In more general situations stockholders will not agree on the objective function of the firm.

value of the firm minus the value of newly issued equities—that is, minus factor costs. For our purpose, it does not matter which method of financing a firm chooses; however, if it chooses to float new equities, it is assumed that a new equity is distinguishable from an old equity so that they can be traded at different prices. The need for this assumption is explained below.

It follows that the net value of an industry (firm) equals its stock market value minus factor costs:

$$(5.2) \qquad V_j^N = V_j - wL_j - rK_j, \qquad j = 1, 2$$

where V_j^N is the net value of industry j, V_j the stock market value of industry j, w the wage rate, and r the physical capital rental rate.

The stock market value of the industry depends on its input choice and on objective market conditions. Hence, an industry can maximize only its perceived net value, which equals its perceived stock market value $V_j(\cdot)$ minus factor costs. The central question is: How does it perceive its stock market value as a function of its decision variables, given the observed market conditions?

Suppose that a firm in sector j has chosen L_j^0 units of labor and K_j^0 units of capital, and that this input choice has resulted in an observed market value of V_j^0. This means that V_j^0 is the stock market evaluation of the random return $R_j^0(\alpha)$ of the firm, where $R_j^0(\alpha) = p_j(\alpha)\theta_j(\alpha)f_j(L_j^0, K_j^0)$, $p_j(\alpha)$ being the price of good j in state α, $\alpha = 1, 2, \ldots, S$. Since the firm is small relative to the market, it assumes that V_j^0 represents the price of the random variable R_j^0, and that it may sell as many units as it wishes of this random variable without influencing its price. In particular, it assumes that if its return is $2R_j^0(\alpha)$ instead of $R_j^0(\alpha)$, its market value will be $2V_j^0$ instead of V_j^0. Under these conditions, the perceived stock market value of the firm is

$$V_j(L_j, K_j) = \frac{V_j^0}{f_j(L_j^0, K_j^0)} f_j(L_j, K_j)$$

The firm is also assumed to be a competitor in factor markets, so that it takes factor prices as given. Hence, the decision problem of the firm can be formulated as

$$(5.3) \qquad \text{choose} \quad L_j, K_j \geq 0$$

$$\text{to maximize}$$

$$\frac{V_j^0}{f_j(L_j^0, K_j^0)} f_j(L_j, K_j) - wL_j - rK_j$$

The decision problem of the industry is identical to that of the firm, and we interpret (5.3) as the decision problem of the industry so that in (5.3) $j = 1, 2$. The solution to (5.3) may be unbounded, which is the usual case for constant returns to scale technologies.

Let L_j^* and K_j^* solve (5.3). The industry is said to be in equilibrium if (L_j^*, K_j^*) solves (5.3) for $L_j^0 = L_j^*$ and $K_j^0 = K_j^*$. Namely, the industry is said to be in equilibrium if at the chosen levels of factor inputs its resulting stock market value is such that it cannot increase its net value by changing its input levels.

This means that in an equilibrium in which every industry operates at a finite level,

(5.4a)
$$\frac{V_j}{f_j(L_j, K_j)} \frac{\partial f_j(L_j, K_j)}{\partial L_j} = w, \qquad j = 1, 2$$

(5.4b)
$$\frac{V_j}{f_j(L_j, K_j)} \frac{\partial f_j(L_j, K_j)}{\partial K_j} = r, \qquad j = 1, 2$$

Using the fact that $f_j(\cdot)$ is homogeneous of degree one, we multiply (5.4a) by L_j, (5.4b) by K_j, and add them up to obtain

(5.5)
$$V_j = wL_j + rK_j, \qquad j = 1, 2$$

Hence, in equilibrium, the stock market value of an industry equals its factor costs—implying that its net value equals zero. This means that when input costs are financed by floating new equities, the value of old equities equals zero. Alternatively, the price of an old share goes to zero, but the price of a new share is positive since $V_j > 0$ is the value of the new shares. This is why we require a distinction between old and new equities.[4]

In what follows, we assume that factor costs are borne directly by the initial stockholders of an industry in proportion to their share of ownership.

---

[4] This distinction is not required if $f_j(\cdot)$ is strictly concave. In this case the equilibrium net value is positive, and we can calculate the number of new equities (which are indistinguishable from old equities) that have to be issued in order to cover factor costs as $(wL_j + rK_j)/(V_j - wL_j - rK_j)$ multiplied by the number of old shares. Observe that this goes to infinity in the case of constant returns to scale.

5.3 CONSUMERS

Consumers are assumed to be endowed with physical capital, labor, and fractions of ownership in firms. Before the resolution of uncertainty, a typical consumer sells his factor endowments (capital and labor) at the going price, and buys or sells ownership fractions in firms. After the resolution of uncertainty, he buys commodities, using his total returns from firm ownerships in the realized state of nature.

We assume that the economy is composed of identical consumers. This enables us to discuss everything in terms of a single aggregate consumer.

Suppose that our (aggregate) consumer owns the share s_1 of the equities of the first industry and the share s_2 of the equities of the second industry. If there is no international trade in securities, both s_1 and s_2 have to be equal to one; that is, each local industry is entirely owned by local residents. However, if there is international trade in securities, then it may happen that $s_1 < 1$ (which means that some of the equities of the first industry are owned by foreigners) and that $s_2 > 1$ (which means that local residents own all equities of the second industry, plus a certain amount of foreign equities which are perfect substitutes for the equities issued by the domestic industry 2).[5] Suppose, for example, that $s_2 = 1.5$. This means that local residents own all of the second industry, plus identical foreign equities equivalent to fifty percent of the equities issued by the local second industry. In any case, in state α these equities provide an income of

$$(5.6) \qquad I(\alpha) = s_1\theta_1(\alpha)f_1(L_1, K_1) + s_2p(\alpha)\theta_2(\alpha)f_2(L_2, K_2)$$

in terms of commodity 1, where

$$p(\alpha) \equiv \frac{p_2(\alpha)}{p_1(\alpha)}$$

is the price of good 2 in terms of good 1 in state α, and (L_1, K_1) and (L_2, K_2) represent the interindustry allocations of labor and capital.

---

[5] In a more general setup, one can introduce domestic equities which do not have perfect substitutes abroad, as well as foreign equities which do not have perfect substitutes at home. There is also no necessary correspondence between goods and types of equities which are issued by industries that produce them.

Naturally, given the realization of state α, the consumer chooses consumption so as to maximize his utility level subject to his budget constraint. Therefore, he solves the following problem in state α:

(5.7)   choose $c_1(\alpha), c_2(\alpha) \geq 0$

to maximize

$u[c_1(\alpha), c_2(\alpha)]$

subject to

$c_1(\alpha) + p(\alpha)c_2(\alpha) \leq I(\alpha)$

where $u(\cdot)$ is the state-independent von Neumann–Morgenstern utility function,[6] and $c_j(\alpha)$ the consumption of commodity j in state α. Let

$$c_j(\alpha) = c_j[p(\alpha), I(\alpha)], \qquad j = 1, 2$$

be the solution to this problem. $c_j[p(\alpha), I(\alpha)]$ is, of course, an ordinary demand function, and we may use it to define the indirect utility function

(5.8) $v[p(\alpha), I(\alpha)] \overset{\text{def}}{=} u\{c_1[p(\alpha), I(\alpha)], c_2[p(\alpha), I(\alpha)]\}$

$$\alpha = 1, 2, \ldots, S$$

$v(\cdot)$ is the highest utility level that the economy (the consumer) can achieve in state α, given the relative price $p(\alpha)$ and income $I(\alpha)$. Thus, the highest utility level that a consumer can reach in state α, for all $\alpha = 1, 2, \ldots, S$, depends on the relative price $p(\alpha)$ which he does not control, on firm inputs and technology which he does not control, and on his portfolio composition (s_1, s_2) which he does control. The consumer chooses his portfolio so as to maximize his expected utility level subject to his assets budget constraint; this constraint is now discussed.

Let the consumer's (economy's) endowment consist of L units of labor, K units of capital, the share $\bar{s}_1 = 1$ of the equities of the first industry, and the share $\bar{s}_2 = 1$ of the equities of the second industry.[7] From sales of labor services and capital services, the consumer receives $wL + rK$ dollars. However, since he has to bear the factor costs of each industry according to his initial ownership share of the equities of

---

[6] $u(\cdot)$ can be made state dependent [as in Kemp and Liviatan (1973)] without affecting our analysis.

[7] The assumption that local industries are initially owned by local residents is natural in a two-period model. This assumption is relaxed in Chapter 11, where we consider a dynamic multiperiod extension.

the industry, the difference between the value of his final portfolio and the value of his initial portfolio should not exceed

$$wL + rK - \sum_{j=1}^{2} \bar{s}_j(wL_j + rK_j)$$

Hence, the consumer's assets budget constraint is

$$V_1 s_1 + V_2 s_2 \leq wL + rK - \sum_{j=1}^{2} \bar{s}_j(wL_j + rK_j) + V_1 \bar{s}_1 + V_2 \bar{s}_2$$

$$= wL + rK + \sum_{j=1}^{2} \bar{s}_j(V_j - wL_j - rK_j)$$

Using this constraint, the portfolio of the economy is determined by the solution to the problem

(5.9)   choose $s_1, s_2 \geq 0$

to maximize

$Ev[p(\alpha), s_1\theta_1(\alpha)f_1(L_1, K_1) + s_2 p(\alpha)\theta_2(\alpha)f_2(L_2, K_2)]$

subject to

$$V_1 s_1 + V_2 s_2 \leq wL + rK + \sum_{j=1}^{2} \bar{s}_j(V_j - wL_j - rK_j)$$

where E is the expectations operator, based on subjective probability beliefs.

Before we go on, it should be mentioned that the state-dependent relative commodity price $p(\alpha)$ is given to the competitive economy by the outside world if there is international trade in commodities. If there is no international trade in commodities, $p(\alpha)$ is endogenous.

5.4   AN ALTERNATIVE SPECIFICATION

Trading in the stock market can be given another interpretation which clarifies the relationship between a stock market economy and an economy without uncertainty.

We argued that a firm in sector j sells on the stock market a random monetary return $R_j(\alpha) \equiv p_j(\alpha)\theta_j(\alpha)f_j(L_j, K_j)$. However, we may also think of sector j as producing and selling on the stock market a product—call it a real equity of type j—which provides commodity j in fixed proportions over all states of nature. More accurately, it provides the monetary value of a quantity of good j in each state of nature. One real equity of type j provides the basket $[\theta_j(1), \theta_j(2), \ldots, \theta_j(S)]$ of commodity j; two units of this real equity provide two such baskets; and so on.

Industry j produces $Z_j = f_j(L_j, K_j)$ real equities of type j. Hence, if N_j is its number of outstanding equities, $N_j/f_j(L_j, K_j)$ of its equities command ownership over one real equity of type j. Since the individual firm is small relative to the market, it takes as given the price of a real equity.

Let q_j be the price of type-j real equities. Then, the perceived stock market value of the jth industry is

$$V_j(L_j, K_j) = q_j Z_j = q_j f_j(L_j, K_j)$$

How do industries know real equity prices? The stock market reveals total industry values for a given output of real equities, and each industry calculates its real equity price by dividing its total value by its activity level. Thus, if industry j chooses to employ $L_j{}^0$ units of labor services and $K_j{}^0$ units of capital services, and it observes that this input choice results in a market value of $V_j{}^0$, then it computes its real equity price as $V_j{}^0/f_j(L_j{}^0, K_j{}^0)$. This means that it supposes that by, say, doubling its output of real equities, it will double its value on the stock market. Therefore, each industry chooses its inputs so as to solve the problem [compare with (5.3)]

(5.10)   choose $L_j, K_j \geq 0$

                                 to maximize

                                 $q_j Z_j - wL_j - rK_j$

                                 subject to

                                 $Z_j = f_j(L_j, K_j)$

This is very similar to profit maximization, and it is well known that the solution to this problem depends only on relative prices (see Chapter 2).

Let us now return to the consumer. When a consumer buys the proportion s_j of the shares of the jth industry, he is actually buying $s_j f_j(L_j, K_j)$ units of real equities. We can therefore transform the consumer's portfolio problem into a problem of real equity purchase.

Let z_j denote the number of real equities held by the consumer, where $z_j = s_j f_j(L_j, K_j)$. Then, using (5.6), the consumer's income in state α can be written as

(5.11) $I(\alpha) = \theta_1(\alpha)z_1 + p(\alpha)\theta_2(\alpha)z_2$

The consumer's decision problem (5.7) need not be transformed, except that now we use (5.11) for income instead of (5.6). Similarly, the definition of the indirect utility function in (5.8) remains valid. However, the consumer's decision problem (5.9)—the portfolio decision problem—has to be adjusted. The objective function remains the maximization of expected utility. But now the consumer has to choose z_1 and z_2 (real equity purchase) instead of s_1 and s_2.

Since $V_j = q_j f_j(L_j, K_j)$ and $s_j = z_j / f_j(L_j, K_j)$, (5.9) can be written in the equivalent form

(5.12)   choose $z_1, z_2 \geq 0$

to maximize

$$Ev[p(\alpha), \theta_1(\alpha)z_1 + p(\alpha)\theta_2(\alpha)z_2]$$

subject to

$$q_1 z_1 + q_2 z_2 \leq wL + rK + \sum_{j=1}^{2} \bar{s}_j [q_j f_j(L_j, K_j) - wL_j - rK_j]$$

5.5 EQUILIBRIUM

In the discussion of equilibrium we have to distinguish between two cases: when there is international trade both in securities and commodities; and when securities are traded only within national borders, but there is international trade in commodities.

In the first case we assume that our (competitive) economy faces given state-dependent commodity prices and given security prices. In the second case the economy faces given state-dependent commodity prices, while security prices are domestically determined. In both cases factor prices are domestically determined, since we assume that there is no international factor movement.

In equilibrium, all domestic markets have to clear. This means that factor prices w and r settle on market clearing levels such that

(5.13a) $L_1 + L_2 = L$

(5.13b) $K_1 + K_2 = K$

In the Ricardian model, r and (5.13b) are meaningless and have to be disregarded.

In addition, if there is no international trade in securities, real equity prices will be determined so as to make domestic investors willing to fully own domestic industries. Namely,

(5.14) $\qquad z_j = Z_j \quad$ (or $\quad s_j = 1$), $\qquad j = 1, 2$

Obviously, in the small-country case, no individual country market clearing condition is required for internationally traded goods and securities. However, for all trading countries taken together, equilibrium commodity prices and equilibrium prices of traded securities have to be such that these markets clear.

Using the fact that $f_j(\cdot)$ is homogeneous of degree one, the net value maximization problem (5.10) of the industry can also be written in the form

(5.15) $\qquad$ choose $a_{Lj}, a_{Kj}, Z_j \geq 0$

to maximize

$Z_j(q_j - wa_{Lj} - ra_{Kj})$

subject to

$f_j(a_{Lj}, a_{Kj}) = 1$

where $a_{Lj} = L_j/Z_j$ is the labor real equity–output ratio and $a_{Kj} = K_j/Z_j$ is the capital real equity–output ratio. This is identical to the problem of an industry in the deterministic Heckscher–Ohlin model, except that here real equities replace commodities (see Chapter 2). In the Ricardian model, (5.15) should be replaced by

(5.16) $\qquad$ choose $Z_j \geq 0$

to maximize

$Z_j(q_j - wa_{Lj})$

where a_{Lj} is the labor real equity–output ratio, and is constant.

From (5.15) we have the well-known results (see Chapter 2)

(5.17a) $\quad Z_j = 0$ $\qquad\qquad$ when $\quad q_j < C_j(w, r)$

(5.17b) $\quad Z_j = [0, +\infty)$ $\qquad$ when $\quad q_j = C_j(w, r)$, $\qquad j = 1, 2$

(5.17c) $\quad Z_j \rightarrow +\infty$ $\qquad\quad$ when $\quad q_j > C_j(w, r)$

where $C_j(\cdot)$ is the minimum cost function of $f_j(\cdot) = 1$; that is, it gives the minimum cost required to produce one real equity of type j at factor prices (w, r).

Similarly, from (5.16), we have for the Ricardian model

(5.18a) $Z_j = 0$ when $q_j < wa_{Lj}$

(5.18b) $Z_j = [0, +\infty)$ when $q_j = wa_{Lj}$

(5.18c) $Z_j \to +\infty$ when $q_j > wa_{Lj}$

Let $q = q_2/q_1$ be the relative price of a type-2 real equity. From Chapter 2, we know that for the Heckscher–Ohlin model there exist functions $\omega(q), \rho(q), Z_j(q, L, K), j = 1, 2$, such that if q is the equilibrium relative price of real equities and q_1 is the absolute price of a type-1 real equity, then the equilibrium supply of real equity j is $Z_j(q, L, K)$, and equilibrium factor prices are

(5.19a) $w = q_1\omega(q)$

(5.19b) $r = q_1\rho(q)$

We also know that for given technologies with different factor intensities, there exist $\underline{q}$ and $\overline{q}$ which depend only on K/L; that is, the aggregate capital–labor ratio, such that $Z_j(q, L, K) > 0$ for $\underline{q} < q < \overline{q}$. The interval $(\underline{q}, \overline{q})$ defines the nonspecialization relative equity prices, and within it $Z_2(\cdot)$ is increasing in q and $Z_1(\cdot)$ is decreasing in q.

$Z_j(\cdot)$ are supply functions along the transformation curve. Hence,

(5.20) $-\dfrac{Z_{1q}(q, L, K)}{Z_{2q}(q, L, K)} \equiv q$ for $q \in (\underline{q}, \overline{q})$

Also, due to the linear homogeneity of the functions $f_j(\cdot), j = 1, 2$, we have in the production equilibrium

(5.21) $wL + rK = q_1\omega(q)L + q_1\rho(q)K$
$$= q_1[Z_1(q, L, K) + qZ_2(q, L, K)]$$

By using (5.21) and the fact that in a production equilibrium the net value of an industry equals zero [see (5.5)], the portfolio problem (5.12) of the economy can be rewritten as

(5.22)   choose $z_1, z_2 \geq 0$

        to maximize

        $Ev[p(\alpha), \theta_1(\alpha)z_1 + p(\alpha)\theta_2(\alpha)z_2]$

        subject to

        $z_1 + qz_2 \leq Z_1(q, L, K) + qZ_2(q, L, K)$

The first-order conditions for an interior solution to this problem are

(5.23a) $$Ev_1(\alpha)\theta_1(\alpha) - \kappa = 0$$

(5.23b) $$Ev_1(\alpha)p(\alpha)\theta_2(\alpha) - \kappa q = 0$$

where $v_1(\alpha)$ is the marginal utility of income in state α, and κ the Lagrangian multiplier of the assets budget constraint. These two conditions reduce to

(5.24) $$Ev_1(\alpha)[p(\alpha)\theta_2(\alpha) - q\theta_1(\alpha)] = 0$$

Since $v_1(\alpha) > 0$ for all $\alpha = 1, 2, \ldots, S$, (5.24) implies that a necessary condition for the economy not to specialize in its portfolio is that the bracketed term in (5.24) equals zero for all $\alpha = 1, 2, \ldots, S$, or that it changes signs over the states of the world at least once.[8]

Suppose there is no international trade in securities. Then, the equilibrium relative price of type-2 real equities is determined so as to equate the demand and supply of each type of real equity. Thus, q^* is the equilibrium-relative price of a type-2 real equity if the solution to (5.22) for $q = q^*$ is z_1^* and z_2^* such that

$$z_1^* = Z_1(q^*, L, K)$$
$$z_2^* = Z_2(q^*, L, K)$$

If there is international trade in securities, q is assumed to be given to our economy. In this case it chooses z_1 and z_2 so as to solve (5.22); this may require imports of one type of real equities, and exports of the other type. This issue is discussed in the next chapter.

At this point the reader should be aware of the fact that our model is consistent with the deterministic model. In fact, if one chooses $\theta_1(\alpha) = \theta_2(\alpha) = 1$ for $\alpha = 1, 2, \ldots, S$, and $p(\alpha) = q$ for all $\alpha = 1, 2, \ldots, S$, then one immediately obtains the well-known deterministic model of international trade.

Before we proceed to the diagrammatic exposition of the stock market equilibrium and the balance of payments, let us repeat the two stages of the consumer's choice problem. In the first stage, before a state of the world realizes, the economy chooses its optimal portfolio by solving (5.22). Then, when the state of the world realizes, it solves the consumption problem (5.7) with income given by (5.11). In the

---

[8] From (5.24), $q = Ev_1(\alpha)\theta_1(\alpha)[p(\alpha)\theta_2(\alpha)/\theta_1(\alpha)]/Ev_1(\alpha)\theta_1(\alpha)$. Hence, q should be a weighted average of $p(\alpha)\theta_2(\alpha)/\theta_1(\alpha)$.

second-stage choice problem, the economy uses an ordinary preference ordering defined on the commodity space. In the first stage, it uses a preference ordering over real equities which is induced by the ordinary preference ordering, probability beliefs, and the distribution of prices. To see this, define

$$(5.25) \qquad U(z_1, z_2 | p) \overset{\text{def}}{=} Ev[p(\alpha), \theta_1(\alpha)z_1 + p(\alpha)\theta_2(\alpha)z_2]$$

$U(\cdot)$ is the utility function over real equities. We call it the assets utility function. The combinations of all (z_1, z_2) which satisfy $U(z_1, z_2 | p) =$ constant is called an assets–indifference curve. The portfolio problem (5.22) can also be written as the maximization of $U(z_1, z_2 | p)$, subject to the assets budget constraint.

We have added p in $U(\cdot)$ in order to remind the reader that preferences over real equities depend on the price distribution. In fact, for two alternative price distributions, say $[p^1(1), p^1(2), \ldots, p^1(S)]$ and $[p^2(1), p^2(2), \ldots, p^2(S)]$, we obtain two different indifference fields in the (z_1, z_2) space. A shift in the price distribution twists the assets–indifference curves in a systematic way.[9]

Equipped with this information, we proceed to the next chapter.

REFERENCES

Arrow, K. J. (1963–1964). The role of securities in the optimal allocation of risk-bearing, *Review of Economic Studies* **34**, 91–96.

Diamond, P. A. (1967). The role of a stock market in a general equilibrium model with technological uncertainty, *American Economic Review* **57**, 759–776.

Ekern, S., and Wilson, R. (1974). On the theory of the firm in an economy with incomplete markets, *Bell Journal of Economics and Management Science* **5**, 171–179.

Hart, O. D. (1974). A model of the stock market with many goods, Research Memorandum No. 165, Princeton Univ., Princeton, New Jersey.

[9] It can be shown that

$$\frac{\partial \text{MRS}}{\partial p(\alpha')} = \text{MRS}\left[\frac{v_{11}(\alpha')}{v_1(\alpha')}c_2(\alpha') + c_{21}(\alpha')\right]$$

$$\times \left[\frac{\pi(\alpha')v_1(\alpha')\theta_2(\alpha')p(\alpha')}{Ev_1(\alpha)\theta_2(\alpha)p(\alpha)} - \frac{\pi(\alpha')v_1(\alpha')\theta_1(\alpha')}{Ev_1(\alpha)\theta_1(\alpha)}\right]$$

where $\text{MRS} = (\partial U/\partial z_1)/(\partial U/\partial z_2)$ is the marginal rate of substitution between z_1 and z_2 along the assets–indifference curve, and $\pi(\alpha)$ is the probability of state α, $v_{11}(\alpha) = \partial v_1(\alpha)/\partial I(\alpha)$ and $c_{21}(\alpha) = \partial c_2(\alpha)/\partial I(\alpha)$.

Hart, O. D. (1975). On the optimality of equilibrium when markets are incomplete, *Journal of Economic Theory* **11**, 418–443.

Helpman, E., and Razin, A. (1978). Participation equilibrium and the efficiency of stock market allocations, *International Economic Review* **19**, 129–140.

Kemp, M. C., and Liviatan, N. (1973). Production and trade patterns under uncertainty, *Economic Record* **42**, 215–227.

Chapter 6

A Diagrammatic Exposition
of Stock Market Equilibrium
and the Balance of Payments

The traditional models of international trade were extended in the previous chapter to an uncertain environment with financial markets. Our simple model can be extended into a many-commodity, many-factors-of-production world with bonds and equities. Here we pursue the simple version.

We develop in this chapter a simple diagrammatic apparatus which enables us to present equilibrium in the stock market before the realization of a state of the world, and equilibrium in commodity trade after the realization of a state of the world. This apparatus is most useful in analyzing the interaction between the two equilibria, which amounts to analyzing the interaction between trade in goods and trade in securities.

What is very important about our diagrammatic exposition is that it uses well-known diagrams from the traditional theory of international trade. We believe this brings out in a clear way the relationship between the traditional theory and its extension as developed in the present study. In the last section of this chapter we show how to modify the diagrams in the presence of a bond.

6.1 THE BASIC PROBLEMS

Before we commence the diagrammatical exposition, it would be convenient to repeat the two basic problems that face the economy: the portfolio problem (5.22) and the consumption problem (5.7).

Before a state of the world realizes, individuals and firms face a distribution of commodity prices, a distribution of technological parameters, equity prices, and prices of factors of production. Given equity prices and prices of factors of production, firms (industries) choose labor and capital inputs so as to maximize their net value. Using this decision rule and factor market clearing conditions, we saw that equilibrium factor prices depend on equity prices [see (5.19)], exactly as in the deterministic model. This enabled us to derive reduced-form supply functions of real equities, $Z_j(q, L, K)$, $j = 1, 2$, which are supply functions *along the transformation curve* between real equity outputs; they depend on the relative price of real equities $q (= q_2/q_1)$ and the endowment by the economy of labor L and capital K. Hence, given q and total factor endowments L and K, industry j will operate at the level Z_j, and it will supply Z_j units of real equities of type j such that

$$(6.1) \qquad\qquad Z_j = Z_j(q, L, K), \qquad j = 1, 2$$

Now, given q and its induced equilibrium factor prices, factor income in terms of real equities of type-1 equals $Z_1(q, L, K) + qZ_2(q, L, K)$ [see (5.21)]. This income provides all resources that can be spent on equity purchase, because the net value of the initial stock holdings of the economy is zero. This is so because the payments by each industry for factors of production exhaust the entire market value of its stocks. Hence, the economy chooses its optimal portfolio by solving [see (5.22) and (5.25)]

(6.2) choose $z_1, z_2 \geq 0$

to maximize

$U(z_1, z_2 | p) \equiv Ev[p(\alpha); \theta_1(\alpha)z_1 + p(\alpha)\theta_2(\alpha)z_2]$

subject to

$z_1 + qz_2 \leq Z_1(q, L, K) + qZ_2(q, L, K)$

In the second stage, after the realization of a state of the world, the economy observes commodity prices and uses the income from its portfolio to choose its optimal consumption bundle. This is done by solving

(6.3)   choose $c_1(\alpha), c_2(\alpha) \geq 0$
              to maximize
              $u[c_1(\alpha), c_2(\alpha)]$
              subject to
              $c_1(\alpha) + p(\alpha)c_2(\alpha) \leq \theta_1(\alpha)z_1 + p(\alpha)\theta_2(\alpha)z_2$

where z_1 and z_2 are the solution to (6.2).

The solution to (6.3) and the supply functions (6.1) determine the optimal trade pattern. This is so because the output of good j in state α is $\theta_j(\alpha)Z_j$, so that optimal exports (imports if negative) of good j are $\theta_j(\alpha)Z_j - c_j(\alpha)$, where $c_j(\alpha)$ solves (6.3).

Finally, observe that q is given to the home country in case there exists international trade in securities. If there is no international trade in securities, q is determined by demand and supply conditions in the stock market. In this case, q^* is an equilibrium relative price if

(6.4) $z_j{}^* = Z_j(q^*, L, K),   j = 1, 2$

where $z_1{}^*$ and $z_2{}^*$ solve (6.2) for $q = q^*$. Observe also that $z_1{}^* = Z_1(q^*, L, K)$ implies $z_2{}^* = Z_2(q^*, L, K)$, and vice versa, due to the assets budget constraint in (6.2) (Walras' law).

Now we are ready to begin the diagrammatic exposition.

6.2 NO INTERNATIONAL TRADE IN SECURITIES

We begin with an economy which is engaged in international trade in commodities, but which does not trade in securities with the rest of the world. This may be the case if, for example, international (financial) capital flows are prohibited by law.

In this case, we may represent the equilibrium in the (domestic) stock market by a well-known diagram (Figure 6.1), which resembles the equilibrium of a closed economy. This resemblance stems from the fact that securities are not traded internationally, so that local demand for real equities has to be satisfied by local firms.

In Figure 6.1, TT represents the transformation curve between real equities Z_1 and Z_2. It can be derived from the supply functions

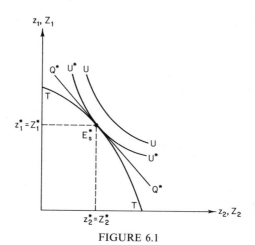

FIGURE 6.1

$Z_j(q, L, K), j = 1, 2$, by varying q in the nonspecialization interval $[\underline{q}, \bar{q}]$ (see Section 5.5). By varying q, the coordinates $[Z_1(q, L, K), Z_2(q, L, K)]$ trace out the transformation curve.

The marginal rate of substitution between Z_2 and Z_1 is $-Z_{1q}(q, L, K)/Z_{2q}(q, L, K)$, and it is identically equal to q [see (5.20)]. Hence, given q, we can obtain the supply level of real equities by finding the point of tangency between the transformation curve TT and a straight line with slope q (a line such as Q^*Q^*).

We can also draw in Figure 6.1 a map of assets–indifference curves. A typical indifference curve represents all combinations of z_1 and z_2 for which $U(z_1, z_2|p) = $ constant. UU and U^*U^* are two representative indifference curves.

The assets–indifference curves are generally convex to the origin, due to the concavity of $v(\cdot)$ in income, which stems from risk aversion. But there is also a case in which these indifference curves become parallel straight lines. This happens when

$$\theta_1(\alpha) = \lambda p(\alpha) \theta_2(\alpha), \qquad \lambda > 0$$

with λ being state independent. In this case,

$$U(z_1, z_2|p) \equiv Ev[p(\alpha); \theta_1(\alpha)(z_1 + \lambda z_2)]$$

and the slope of every assets–indifference curve is λ. This means that the two real equities are perfect substitutes in the investor's portfolio, so that we have, in effect, only one type of security. This is particularly the case in a deterministic environment, since then $\theta_1(\alpha) = \theta_2(\alpha) = 1$, and $p(\alpha) = p$ for all α, which makes the slope of the assets–indifference curves equal to the relative commodity price p. Bearing this fact in mind, the reader will be able to see the relationship between our analysis and the standard deterministic model, since for $\theta_1(\alpha) = \theta_2(\alpha) = 1$ and $p(\alpha) = p$ for all α, our model reduces to the standard (deterministic) model.

The equilibrium in the stock market—that is, the solution to (6.2) with q^* which satisfies (6.4)—obtains at a point of tangency between the highest assets–indifference curve and the real-equity transformation curve. E_s^* is such an equilibrium point, and U^*U^* represents the assets–indifference curve which provides the highest achievable expected utility level. The slope of Q^*Q^*—the tangent line to TT and U^*U^* at E_s^*—is q^*, the domestic equilibrium relative price of real-equity Z_2. At this price, net value maximizing producers supply Z_1^* and Z_2^* real equities, while expected utility maximizing consumers demand z_1^* and z_2^* real equities. Since $z_1^* = Z_1^*$ and $z_2^* = Z_2^*$—that is, the demand for each type of real equity equals its supply—E_s^* represents equilibrium in the stock market.

Figures 6.2 and 6.3 represent the balance of trade in two states of the world: Figure 6.2 for state 1 and Figure 6.3 for state 2.

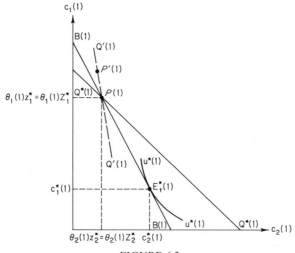

FIGURE 6.2

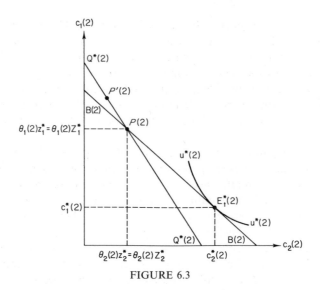

FIGURE 6.3

The portfolio composition determines the consumer's budget line in each state of the world: $B(1)B(1)$ in Figure 6.2 for state 1, and $B(2)B(2)$ in Figure 6.3 for state 2. Obviously, the budget line in state α is given by the equation

$$c_1 + p(\alpha)c_2 = \theta_1(\alpha)z_1{}^* + p(\alpha)\theta_2(\alpha)z_2{}^*$$

Hence, the slope of the budget line $B(\alpha)B(\alpha)$ is $p(\alpha)$, and the point $P(\alpha)$ defined by the coordinates $[\theta_1(\alpha)z_1{}^*, \theta_2(\alpha)z_2{}^*]$ has to lie on the budget line $B(\alpha)B(\alpha)$. Note that in this case (of no international trade in securities) the point $[\theta_1(\alpha)Z_1{}^*, \theta_2(\alpha)Z_2{}^*]$ also lies on the budget line $B(\alpha)B(\alpha)$, and it coincides with $P(\alpha)$. This will not be the case if international trade in securities takes place.

The optimal consumption point in state α is indicated by $E_t{}^*(\alpha)$; the point at which an ordinary indifference curve is tangent to the budget line. The optimal consumption bundle in state α is $[c_1{}^*(\alpha), c_2{}^*(\alpha)]$.

Observe that the way in which Figures 6.2 and 6.3 are drawn implies that the second commodity is imported in both states of the world. This, however, need not be the case; there may be situations in which a country imports a commodity in one state of the world and exports the same commodity in another state of the world. In state α, the economy imports $c_2{}^*(\alpha) - \theta_2(\alpha)Z_2{}^*$ of good 2 and exports $\theta_1(\alpha)Z_1{}^* - c_1{}^*(\alpha)$ of good 1. The trade account is balanced in every state of the world; the value of imports equals the value of exports in every state of the world. The trade account is balanced because there is no international trade in securities, and this necessitates zero capital and service accounts.

The slope of $Q^*(\alpha)Q^*(\alpha)$ in Figures 6.2 and 6.3—the translation of Q^*Q^* from Figure 6.1 to Figures 6.2 and 6.3—is $q^*\theta_1(\alpha)/\theta_2(\alpha)$. $Q^*(\alpha)Q^*(\alpha)$ describes the possible precommodity-trade endowments that the consumer can obtain by portfolio reallocation at constant real equity prices. Naturally, the consumer cannot choose a point on $Q^*(1)Q^*(1)$ independently of his choice of a point on $Q^*(2)Q^*(2)$, because his choice of z_1 and z_2 uniquely determines the points on $Q^*(1)Q^*(1)$ and $Q^*(2)Q^*(2)$.

If there are only two states of the world, the $Q^*(\alpha)Q^*(\alpha)$ line must be steeper than the $B(\alpha)B(\alpha)$ line in one state of the world and flatter in the other state of the world, as shown in Figures 6.2 and 6.3. More generally, the slope of $Q^*(\alpha)Q^*(\alpha)$ minus the slope of $B(\alpha)B(\alpha)$ has to change signs over the states of the world if the portfolio choice problem has an interior solution [see (5.24)]. To see this, assume for a moment that $Q'(1)Q'(1)$ replaces $Q^*(1)Q^*(1)$ in Figure 6.2. Then, by reallocating his portfolio in favor of z_1, the consumer can move his precommodity-trade endowments to a point such as $P'(1)$ on $Q'(1)Q'(1)$ in state 1 (Figure 6.2) and $P'(2)$ on $Q(2)Q(2)$ in state 2 (Figure 6.3). In this situation, his budget line in every state α will be a line which parallels $B(\alpha)B(\alpha)$ and passes through $P'(\alpha)$ (these budget lines are not shown in our figures). It is easy to see that this portfolio reallocation enables the consumer to reach a higher utility level in every state of the world, contradicting the assumption that $(z_1{}^*, z_2{}^*)$ is the optimal portfolio choice. The reader can verify that the slope of $Q^*(\alpha)Q^*(\alpha)$ is larger (smaller) than the slope of $B(\alpha)B(\alpha)$ in every state of the world only if the consumer specializes in z_1 (z_2) in his portfolio.

At this point it is interesting to compare our model to those of Kemp and Liviatan (1973), Turnovsky (1974), Ruffin (1974), and Anderson and Riley (1976). Those authors did not present their models in the framework of an economy with financial markets (except for Kemp and Liviatan who considered Arrow–Debreu contingent commodity markets). However, it is clear from this section and Section 4.3 that their models can be interpreted as models with domestic stock markets but no international trade in securities. Hence, our results concerning economies which do not engage in international trade in equities also apply to their models.

6.3   INTERNATIONAL TRADE IN SECURITIES

Let the economy open to international trade in securities (that is, real equities), and assume that the economy is a price-taker in the international capital market. Assume also for simplicity that commodity prices do not change as a result of trade in securities. No portfolio reallocation will take place if the international price of z_2 (in terms of z_1) equals q^*, the slope of Q^*Q^* in Figure 6.1. Assume, therefore, that the international relative price of z_2 is q and that $q < q^*$.

In Figure 6.4 TT and E_s^* are reproduced from Figure 6.1. The slope of QQ is q, the international relative price of type-2 real equities, and E_{sp} is the net market value maximizing production point at this relative price. E_{sp} lies to the left of E_s^* (on TT) because q is smaller than q^*. Local producers supply Z_1 units of type-1 real equities and Z_2 units of type-2 real equities. Expected utility maximizing consumers choose E_{sc} as their portfolio point, where E_{sc} is the point of tangency between the highest affordable assets–indifference curve UU and the assets–budget line QQ. Local consumers demand z_1 units of type-1 real equities and z_2 units of type-2 real equities. Hence, the opening of the economy to international trade in securities causes our country to exchange with the rest of the world $Z_1 - z_1$ units of type-1 equities for $z_2 - Z_2$ units of type-2 equities (the direction of trade in securities would have been reversed if q was larger that q^*).

Figures 6.5 and 6.6 represent the new balance of payments (trade

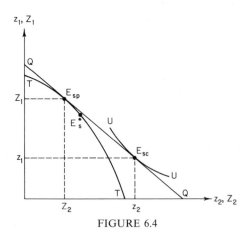

FIGURE 6.4

and service accounts) position in the two states of the world—Figure 6.5 for state 1 and Figure 6.6 for state 2.

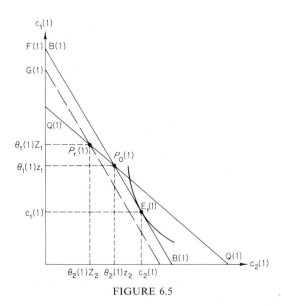

FIGURE 6.5

   Points $P_r(\alpha)$ and $P_0(\alpha)$, the production and the portfolio points, are the translations of E_{sp} and E_{se}, respectively, from Figure 6.4. Both lie on the $Q(\alpha)Q(\alpha)$ line whose slope is now $q\theta_1(\alpha)/\theta_2(\alpha)$. The consumer's budget line $B(\alpha)B(\alpha)$, the slope of which is $p(\alpha)$, passes through $P_0(\alpha)$, the portfolio point, because the consumer's ex-post income derives from the return on his portfolio. The reader should observe that, compared to Figures 6.2 and 6.3 (the case of no international trade in securities), we here have two points $P_r(\alpha)$ and $P_0(\alpha)$ instead of one point $P(\alpha)$. This results from the fact that in the absence of international trade in securities, the production and the portfolio points coincide. Observe that here, too, the slope of $Q(\alpha)Q(\alpha)$ minus the slope of $B(\alpha)B(\alpha)$ changes signs over the states whenever the country does not specialize in its portfolio. It should, however, be clear that when there exist foreign assets with the same structure of returns as the domestic equities, and foreigners hold these assets in their portfolios, then the slope of $Q(\alpha)Q(\alpha)$ minus the slope of $B(\alpha)B(\alpha)$ cannot be sign preserving over the states of the world.

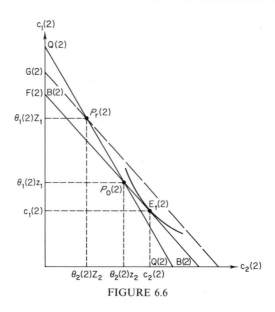

FIGURE 6.6

The optimal consumption point in state α is $E_t(\alpha)$. The country exports $\theta_1(\alpha)Z_1 - c_1(\alpha)$ units of good 1 and imports $c_2(\alpha) - \theta_2(\alpha)Z_2$ units of good 2 in state α. (For simplicity, we have chosen to have it import good 2 in both states of the world.) However, since $P_r(\alpha)$ does not lie on $B(\alpha)B(\alpha)$, the value of imports is *not* equal to the value of exports. In particular, since $P_r(1)$ lies below $B(1)B(1)$, the economy runs a deficit in the balance of trade in state 1; and, since $P_r(2)$ lies above $B(2)B(2)$, the economy runs a surplus in the balance of trade in state 2. Naturally, a deficit in the trade account is financed here by the excess of dividend receipts from abroad over dividend payments to foreigners, and conversely for a surplus. The reader can verify that even if the economy specializes in its portfolio, it never runs a surplus in the trade account of all states, but it may run a deficit in all states. A surplus in all states means that the economy gives foreigners a random gift in all states of nature. Put differently, it engages in an unfavorable gamble, and this is not rational. Observe, however, that the considerations that prevent our country from running a surplus in its trade account in all states of nature prevent also other countries from doing it. Hence, in an equilibrium of the world economy no country is able to run a deficit in its trade account in all states of nature because one country's deficit is another country's surplus. That is, there is no free lunch.

The value of net dividend receipts from abroad in terms of the export good, good 1, is given in state α by $F(\alpha)$ minus $G(\alpha)$, where the dashed line that passes through $P_r(\alpha)$ parallels $B(\alpha)B(\alpha)$. This represents the difference between the value of the portfolio point and the production point evaluated by commodity prices. It is also possible to construct examples in which a country imports all commodities in a particular state of the world and/or exports all commodities in another state of the world.

6.4 STOCK MARKET EQUILIBRIUM WITH A SAFE BOND

A safe bond is a security whose return is state independent. But in our framework, in which relative commodity prices vary across states of nature, fixed returns in terms of commodity 1 mean variable returns in terms of commodity 2, and vice versa. Since there is no money in this system, we have to fix the return on a bond in terms of one of the commodities, or in terms of a fixed bundle of goods.

One can, in fact, introduce two safe bonds—one in terms of commodity 1 and one in terms of commodity 2. This will be equivalent to the existence of future commodity markets, in which contracts are made for the delivery of a good in the contracted amount, independent of the state of nature, but in which payments are made at the time of contracting. However, the introduction of two bonds will not enable a diagrammatic exposition of stock market equilibrium. We therefore introduce only one safe bond, and choose it to provide a safe return in terms of commodity 1. We also choose its units so that one bond provides the value of one unit of good 1 in every state of the world. b is the number of bond holdings (b can be positive or negative), and q_b its price in terms of type-1 real equities.

Now the portfolio problem is [compare it with (6.2)]

(6.5)   choose $z_1, z_2 \geq 0$ and b

to maximize

$$U(z_1, z_2, b \mid p) \equiv Ev[p(\alpha); \theta_1(\alpha)z_1 + p(\alpha)\theta_2(\alpha)z_2 + b]$$

subject to

$$z_1 + qz_2 + q_b b \leq Z_1(q, L, K) + qZ_2(q, L, K)$$

Given asset prices q and q_b, the efficient portfolio possibility frontier is represented in Figure 6.7 by the displaced cone DAE. This cone is tangent to the real equity transformation curve TT at point P_r; that is, $0B$ divided by $0C$ equals q. In addition, $0B$ divided by $0A$ equals q_b.

We can also draw three-dimensional assets–indifference surfaces in Figure 6.7. An indifference surface will represent all combinations of (z_1, z_2, b) for which $U(z_1, z_2, b|p)$ is constant. These indifference surfaces are convex to the origin. The optimal portfolio composition [the solution to (6.5)] can be represented by a point on DAE at which an assets–indifference surface is tangent to DAE.

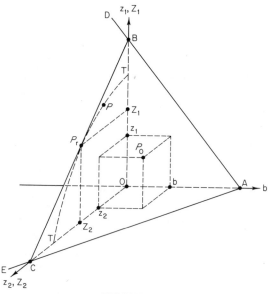

FIGURE 6.7

Let us start with the case in which there is international trade in all securities. In this case, q and q_b are given to our economy and so is DAE. Let P_0 in Figure 6.7 be the point of tangency between an asset–indifference surface and DAE. Then, the coordinates of P_0, (z_1, z_2, b), give the optimal portfolio composition. The coordinates of P_r, $(Z_1, Z_2, 0)$, give the equilibrium (and optimal) production of securities.

Figure 6.7 describes an equilibrium in which the home country has positive bond holdings and exports both types of real equities. In this case it pays for the bonds with both types of real equities. This is, of course, not a necessary outcome; there may be equilibria in which the country exports one of the real equities, imports the others, and has either positive or negative bond holdings. Observe, however, that in the presence of bonds, both local industries may be partially (or wholly) owned by foreigners, or local residents may have some foreign shares and fully own local industries. These possibilities do not arise in the absence of bonds, unless we consider a dynamic setting in which stocks of financial assets are built up by means of trade and savings (see Chapter 11).

Suppose now that there is no international trade in securities. How will security prices be determined?

In this case, the efficient portfolio possibility frontier is the transformation curve TT. Equilibrium obtains at a point of tangency between TT and an indifference surface. Suppose this happens at P. Then, we can draw a displaced cone such as DAE which passes through P and which is tangent to both TT and the indifference surface that passes through P. The slopes of this cone give us the equilibrium asset prices.

We have described here a case in which all securities are internationally traded, and a case in which no security is traded internationally. It is also possible to describe cases in which some securities are traded internationally while others are not; we abstain from doing so here because it is not needed for our arguments in the following chapters.

REFERENCES

Anderson, J., and Riley, T. G. (1976). International trade with fluctuating prices, *International Economic Review* **17**, 79–97.

Kemp, M. C., and Liviatan, N. (1973). Production and trade patterns under uncertainty, *Economic Record* **49**, 215–227.

Ruffin, R. J. (1974). Competitive advantage under uncertainty, *Journal of International Economics* **4**, 261–274.

Turnovsky, S. J. (1974). Technological and price uncertainty in a Ricardian model of international trade, *Review of Economic Studies* **47**, 201–217.

Chapter 7

The Basic Propositions
of the Pure Theory
# of International Trade Revised

It is explained in the survey of the literature (see Chapter 4) that the introduction of uncertainty elements into the economic system may have devastating effects on many of the basic theorems of standard international trade theory. However, that literature has not considered markets for risk sharing. It is therefore important to reassess the fate of these theorems in a world of uncertainty when risk-sharing arrangements are allowed to take place.

When stock markets exist in situations of uncertainty, factor allocations are determined by real equity prices and factor endowments—not directly by commodity prices. The links between the competitive allocation of factors of production and commodity prices are real equity prices; these depend not only on commodity prices but also on risk attitudes and probability assessments. International risk sharing, such as international trade in equities, will equalize real equity prices between countries; in the absence of international trade in equities, real equity prices may not be equalized, even though trade in commodities will equalize commodity prices. Therefore, basic trade theorems such as factor-price equalization are expected to hold under uncertainty if international trade in equities is allowed to take place, but not to hold if international trade in equities does not take place.

Using the model of international trade in goods and securities and the diagrammatic apparatus developed in Chapters 5 and 6, we shall reformulate the central theorems of the pure theory of international trade to accommodate elements of uncertainty. We explain why the basic trade theorems—specialization according to comparative advantage, factor-price equalization, Stolper–Samuelson and Rybczynski— do not carry over to uncertain environments in the absence of international trade in equities and why the Heckscher–Ohlin theorem is upset by uncertainty regardless of whether international trade in equities takes place. We also show that the theorems of specialization according to comparative advantage and factor-price equalization are restored in the presence of international trade in equities, and that there exist valid versions of the Stolper–Samuelson and Rybczynski theorems.

For expositional simplicity we analyze a model with two factors, two equities, and two commodities. However, recent extensions of the standard theorems of international trade to a world of many commodities and many factors of production (Ethier, 1974; Jones and Scheinkman, 1977) carry over to our model if international trade in equities is allowed to take place. The results of a many-commodity Ricardian world apply here as well.

7.1 COMPARATIVE COSTS THEORY

The comparative costs theory (which suggests that each country will specialize in the production and export of the commodity with the lowest relative labor costs) fails to hold when there is no international trade in equities. The reason is that the equilibrium production vector will then depend on preferences and subjective probability beliefs, in addition to relative commodity prices and output–labor ratios; the technological and price risks of the country will be fully borne by local residents, and production decisions could not be separated from preferences, including risk attitudes.

Figure 7.1 shows a typical single-country production equilibrium when international trade in equities does not take place. TT is the Ricardian production possibilities curve of the home country, and UU its highest affordable assets–indifference curve. E_s represents a stock market equilibrium in which the country is incompletely specialized.

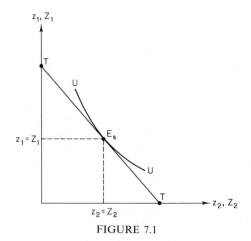

FIGURE 7.1

Now, suppose that we open the economy to trade in equities and assume that countries have the same distributions of $\theta_j(\alpha)$, so that they produce the same real equities. The stock market equilibrium of the home country in the presence of international trade in equities is described in Figure 7.2. Observe that the assets–indifference curves in Figure 7.2 are generally different from the assets–indifference curves in Figure 7.1, for the introduction of trade in securities changes generally the equilibrium distribution of commodity prices, and the

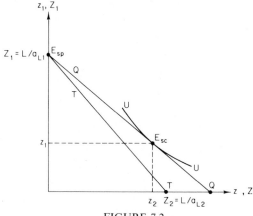

FIGURE 7.2

assets–indifference map depends on the distribution of commodity prices.

The slope of the assets–budget line QQ is q—the relative world price of real equity 2. E_{sp} is the producers' equilibrium point, which indicates a complete specialization in the production of commodity 1 and type-1 real equities. E_{sc} is the domestic investors' equilibrium point. The economy imports z_2 units of type-2 real equities, and exports $L/a_{L1} - z_1$ units of type-1 real equities. Therefore, if international trade in equities takes place, each country specializes according to its comparative advantage—which is well defined by output–input ratios, given that the countries have the same distribution of $\theta_j(\alpha)$.

We now give a two-country example in which in the absence of international trade in equities each country specializes in the commodity in which it has a comparative disadvantage. It is clear from our previous discussion that specialization according to comparative advantage will be restored with the introduction of trade in equities.

EXAMPLE 7.1   Let the utility function of the home country be

$$(7.1) \qquad u(c_1, c_2) = \log(c_1 + \log c_2)$$

and that of the foreign country be (asterisks denote variables of the foreign country)

$$(7.2) \qquad u^*(c_1{}^*, c_2{}^*) = \gamma[(c_1{}^*)^{1/2}(c_2{}^*)^{1/2}]^\mu$$
$$\mu = \tfrac{1}{4}\log 1.1, \quad \gamma > 0$$

Hence, both countries are risk averse.

These utility functions yield the demand and indirect utility functions (with an appropriate choice of γ)

$$(7.3a) \qquad c_1 = I - 1$$

$$(7.3b) \qquad c_2 = \frac{1}{p}$$

$$(7.3c) \qquad v = \log(I - 1 - \log p)$$

$$(7.4a) \qquad c_1{}^* = I^*/2$$

$$(7.4b) \qquad c_2{}^* = I^*/2p$$

$$(7.4c) \qquad v^* = p^{-\mu/2}(I^*)^\mu$$

where p is the relative price of the second commodity and I stands for income, that is, $I = \theta_1 z_1 + p\theta_2 z_2$.

Let a_{Li} and a_{Li}^*, $i = 1, 2$, be the labor–output ratio of the ith industry. We assume that the home country has a comparative advantage in commodity 2, that is,

(7.5)
$$\frac{a_{L2}}{a_{L1}} < \frac{a_{L2}^*}{a_{L1}^*}$$

We choose

(7.6) $a_{L2} = 19, \qquad a_{L1} = 72, \qquad L = 72$

(7.7) $a_{L2}^* = 20, \qquad a_{L1}^* = 72, \qquad L^* = 40$

Assume that there are two states of the world with equal probabilities

(7.8) $\pi(1) = \pi(2) = \tfrac{1}{2}$

These are both objective and subjective probabilities for each country.

We assume also that each country has the same distributions of the technological parameters, which are

(7.9a) $\theta_1(1) = 2, \qquad \theta_1(2) = 5$

(7.9b) $\theta_2(1) = e^9, \qquad \theta_2(2) = e$

We show now that there is an equilibrium of the world economy in which there is no trade in equities and in which the home country specializes in the production of the first commodity while the foreign country specializes in the production of the second commodity, contrary to comparative advantage.

To see this, consider the allocation of resources

(7.10a) $z_1 = Z_1 = \dfrac{L}{a_{L1}} = 1, \qquad z_2 = Z_2 = 0$

(7.10b) $z_1^* = Z_1^* = 0, \qquad z_2^* = Z_2^* = \dfrac{L^*}{a_{L2}^*} = 2$

This implies, using (7.3) and (7.4), the following equilibrium condition in commodity markets in state α (using only the market for good 2):

$$c_2(\alpha) + c_2^*(\alpha) = \frac{1}{p(\alpha)} + \theta_2(\alpha)$$

$$= \theta_2(\alpha)(Z_2 + Z_2^*)$$

$$= 2\theta_2(\alpha)$$

which yields

(7.11)
$$p(\alpha) = \frac{1}{\theta_2(\alpha)}, \qquad \alpha = 1, 2$$

The marginal rates of substitution between assets, evaluated at the allocation (7.10) and equilibrium prices (7.11), are given by

(7.12) $$MRS \equiv \frac{Ev_i(\alpha)\theta_2(\alpha)p(\alpha)}{Ev_i(\alpha)\theta_1(\alpha)}$$

$$= \frac{E[\theta_1(\alpha)z_1 + p(\alpha)\theta_2(\alpha)z_2 - 1 - \log p(\alpha)]^{-1}\theta_2(\alpha)p(\alpha)}{E[\theta_1(\alpha)z_1 + p(\alpha)\theta_2(\alpha)z_2 - 1 - \log p(\alpha)]^{-1}\theta_1(\alpha)}$$

$$= \frac{18}{72}$$

(7.13) $$MRS^* = \frac{E[p(\alpha)]^{-\mu/2}[\theta_1(\alpha)z_1^* + p(\alpha)\theta_2(\alpha)z_2^*]^{\mu-1}p(\alpha)\theta_2(\alpha)}{E[p(\alpha)]^{-\mu/2}[\theta_1(\alpha)z_1^* + p(\alpha)\theta_2(\alpha)z_2^*]^{\mu-1}\theta_1(\alpha)}$$

$$= \frac{21}{72}$$

Hence, for

(7.14)
$$q = \frac{18}{72} < \frac{a_{L2}}{a_{L1}} < \frac{a_{L2}^*}{a_{L1}^*} < q^* = \frac{21}{72}$$

producers and investors choose the equilibrium values given in (7.10), as shown in Figure 7.3.

The equilibrium consumption levels are

(7.15a) $c_1(\alpha) = \theta_1(\alpha) - 1$ $\Rightarrow$ $c_1(1) = 1,$ $c_1(2) = 4$

(7.15b) $c_2(\alpha) = \theta_2(\alpha)$ $\Rightarrow$ $c_2(1) = e^9,$ $c_2(2) = e$

(7.16a) $c_1^*(\alpha) = p(\alpha)\theta_2(\alpha)$ $\Rightarrow$ $c_1^*(1) = 1,$ $c_1^*(2) = 1$

(7.16b) $c_2^*(\alpha) = \theta_2(\alpha)$ $\Rightarrow$ $c_2^*(1) = e^9$ $c_2^*(2) = e$

These values are, of course, consistent with the commodity market clearing conditions. This completes the example.

So far we have discussed identical distributions of the technological parameters, which means that technological uncertainty is industry specific but not country specific. It may, of course, happen that two countries have different distributions of $\theta_j(\alpha)$. In this case they produce

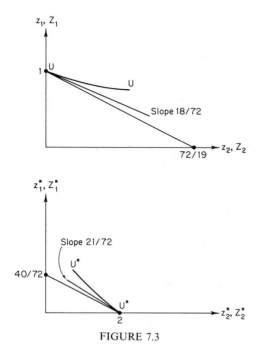

FIGURE 7.3

different real equities while producing the *same commodities.* International trade in goods and securities will not lead to specialization in production if there exists a positive world demand for all securities. Furthermore, a country need not export that commodity in which its input–output ratio is lowest. However, we argue that in this case comparative advantage should be defined with respect to real equities— and, thus, a country exports that real equity in which comparative costs are lowest.

7.2 FACTOR-PRICE EQUALIZATION

The factor-price equalization theorem is fundamental to the Heckscher–Ohlin theory of international trade. It suggests that (under certain conditions) free trade in commodities is sufficient to cause factor prices to be equalized between countries even if there are no world markets for factors of production. This theorem fails to hold under uncertainty in the absence of international trade in securities.

In order to ensure factor-price equalization in our model, one has to ensure that the relative price of type-2 real equities, q, is equalized among the trading countries. But trade in commodities does not bring about equalization of q even in the case in which the traditional conditions for factor-price equalization, such as the absence of specialization and factor intensity reversals, hold. Consider, for example, two trading countries which are identical in all respects, except that the second country has more physical capital than the first. Let the stock market equilibrium of the first country be described by E_s^1 in Figure 7.4.

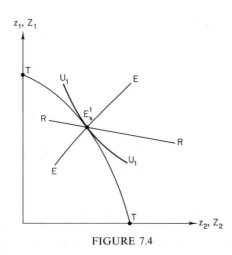

FIGURE 7.4

Clearly, if the Rybczynski line for capital changes, RR, does not coincide with the wealth–portfolio line EE of the second country which passes through E_s^1—where the wealth–portfolio line is the collection of optimal portfolio points for given relative real equity prices and different levels of wealth (i.e., the asset space counterpart of the income-consumption line)—the stock market equilibrium of the second country would consist of a different relative price of type-2 real equities—and, thus, factor prices will not be equalized. Differences in tastes, attitudes toward risk, and subjective probability beliefs may also prevent factor-price equalization.

This does not mean that factor-price equalization is never expected to hold. For if the assets–indifference curves of both countries are linear with the same slope, then factor-price equalization will obtain. Neutrality toward risk by both countries makes their assets–indif-

ference curves linear but not necessarily with the same slope, unless
their ordinal preferences are the same. But even if countries exhibit
risk aversion, the equilibrium distribution of prices may be such as to
make the assets–indifference curves linear with the same slope.

Consider, for example, the case in which two countries have Cobb–
Douglas-type utility functions which exhibit different degrees of risk
aversion. The ordinal preferences may also differ. Given identical
technologies, the equilibrium price distribution is in this case such that
the vector $[p(1)\theta_2(1), p(2)\theta_2(2), \ldots, p(S)\theta_2(S)]$ is proportional to the
vector $[\theta_1(1), \theta_1(2), \ldots, \theta_1(S)]$. This means that in the equilibrium the
two types of equities—real equity 1 and real equity 2—are perfect
substitutes in the investor's portfolio, implying straight-line assets–
indifference curves with a slope equal to the factor of proportionality
between the two vectors. Hence, both countries have the same straight-
line assets–indifference field, implying factor-price equalization under
the standard conditions.

First, let us show that proportionality of the two vectors implies
straight-line assets–indifference curves, with a slope equal to the factor
of proportionality, for every utility function. Suppose that

(7.17) $\theta_2(\alpha)p(\alpha) = \lambda\theta_1(\alpha), \qquad \alpha = 1, 2, \ldots, S, \quad \lambda > 0$

Then

$$\begin{aligned}
\text{MRS} &\equiv \frac{Ev_1(\alpha)\theta_2(\alpha)p(\alpha)}{Ev_1(\alpha)\theta_1(\alpha)} \\
&= \frac{Ev_1(\alpha)\lambda\theta_1(\alpha)}{Ev_1(\alpha)\theta_1(\alpha)} \\
&= \lambda
\end{aligned}$$

Second, let us show that (7.17) is implied by Cobb–Douglas utility
functions. Let the utility functions be

(7.18) $u = (c_1^{1-\beta}c_2^{\beta})^{\mu}, \qquad 0 < \beta, \quad \mu < 1$

(7.19) $u^* = [(c_1^*)^{1-\beta^*}(c_2^*)^{\beta^*}]^{\mu^*}, \qquad 0 < \beta^*, \quad \mu^* < 1$

Then, the market clearing condition for good 2 in state α is

(7.20) $\beta[\theta_1(\alpha)z_1 + p(\alpha)\theta_2(\alpha)z_2] + \beta^*[\theta_1(\alpha)z_1^* + p(\alpha)\theta_2(\alpha)z_2^*]$
$= p(\alpha)\theta_2(\alpha)(Z_2 + Z_2^*)$

It is clear from (7.20) that (7.17) holds with

$$(7.21) \qquad \lambda = \frac{\beta z_1 + \beta^* z_1^*}{Z_2 + Z_2^* - \beta z_2 - \beta^* z_2^*}, \qquad \lambda > 0$$

since $Z_2 + Z_2^* = z_2 + z_2^*$ and $0 < \beta,\ \beta^* < 1$. The Cobb–Douglas result holds also in a many-commodity world, as one can easily verify.

We have thus shown that in the case of Cobb–Douglas-type ordinal preferences, factor-price equalization holds under the standard conditions if there is no international trade in securities. Now, suppose that we open the economies to trade in real equities. Then, for general utility functions, if countries have the same distribution of $\theta_j(\alpha)$, $j = 1, 2$, that is, technological uncertainty is industry specific and not country specific (this is the generalization under uncertainty of the assumption of identical production technologies between countries), then independent of preferences, factor-price equalization will hold. International trade in equities will equalize relative real-equity prices across countries, and thus is sufficient to cause factor prices to be equalized under the standard conditions.

In the Heckscher–Ohlin model, commodity trade serves as a substitute for factor movements if countries do not specialize; this is due to the factor-price equalization theorem. However, it is clear from our discussion that in the presence of uncertainty, commodity trade does not substitute for factor movements—but trade in goods *and* securities does substitute for factor movements, provided the distribution of $\theta_j(\alpha)$, $j = 1, 2$, is the same in the trading countries in addition to the other assumptions. That is if the conditions of the theorem are satisfied, the opening of international markets for factors of production will not induce international factor flows (Mundell, 1957).

It is important at this point to recognize the strength of the assumptions which assure factor-price equalization in the presence of international trade in equities. Apart from the standard Heckscher–Ohlin-type assumptions, it is required that countries have identical sectoral-specific perfectly correlated technological uncertainty. Thus, if India and the United States both produce the same crop, then not only do they have to have the same density function of rainfall, but also that when in fact 66.9 inches of rain falls in the United States, then exactly 66.9 inches of rain falls in India. This means that we can hardly expect factor-price equalization even in the presence of trade in equities. Clearly, if there is no trade in equities (or for this matter even some equities), then even under very strong assumptions factor-price equalization cannot be expected to take place.

7.3   THE STOLPER–SAMUELSON THEOREM

The Stolper–Samuelson theorem asserts that in the Heckscher–Ohlin model an increase in the price of a commodity induces an increase in the real reward of the factor in which this industry is relatively intensive, and a reduction in the reward of the other factor of production. Let us consider this theorem in the present framework.

Assume, first, that international trade in equities does not take place. For simplicity, consider a small country that faces state-independent commodity prices (that is, which are not subject to uncertainty). The production technology, however, is state dependent. Let E_s in Figure 7.5 describe the stock market equilibrium of the country, at which the highest affordable assets–indifference curve UU is reached.

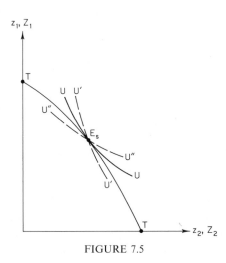

FIGURE 7.5

Suppose that the relative price of the second commodity rises. This shifts the entire assets–indifference map. In general, the marginal rates of substitution between type-1 and type-2 real equities and the assets–indifference curves pivot as a result of the increase in the relative price of good 2.

If the new assets–indifference curve which passes through E_s is steeper than UU at E_s, as described by $U'U'$, the relative price of type-2 real equities will rise—thereby inducing an increase in the real reward (in terms of real equities) of the factor that is used more intensively in the second industry. This is the Stolper–Samuelson theorem.

However, if the new assets–indifference curve that passes through E_s is flatter than UU at E_s, as described by $U''U''$, the relative price of type-2 real equities will fall—and the prediction of the Stolper–Samuelson theorem will turn out to be wrong.

The following example demonstrates a situation in which the Stolper–Samuelson theorem does not hold.

EXAMPLE 7.2   Let the utility function be

(7.22) $$u = \log(c_2 + \log c_1)$$

This yields the indirect utility function

(7.23) $$v = \log\left(\frac{I}{p} - 1 + \log p\right)$$

which implies

(7.24) $$\mathrm{MRS} \equiv \frac{Ev_1(\alpha)p(\alpha)\theta_2(\alpha)}{Ev_1(\alpha)\theta_1(\alpha)}$$

$$= \frac{E[\theta_1(\alpha)p(\alpha)^{-1}z_1 + \theta_2(\alpha)z_2 - 1 + \log p(\alpha)]^{-1}\theta_2(\alpha)}{E[\theta_1(\alpha)p(\alpha)^{-1}z_1 + \theta_2(\alpha)z_2 - 1 + \log p(\alpha)]^{-1}\theta_1(\alpha)p(\alpha)^{-1}}$$

Assume now that $\theta_2(\alpha) = 1$ for all α, $p(\alpha) = p$ for all α, and that at the initial equilibrium

$$z_1 = z_2 = p = 1$$

This choice of real-equity holdings can be assured by an appropriate choice of production technologies and factor endowments. Then, the derivative of MRS with respect to p, evaluated at the initial equilibrium, is

$$\frac{\partial \mathrm{MRS}}{\partial p} = E\frac{1}{\theta_1(\alpha)} - \left[E\left(\frac{1}{\theta_1(\alpha)}\right)^2 - \left(E\frac{1}{\theta_1(\alpha)}\right)^2\right]$$

$$= E\frac{1}{\theta_1(\alpha)} - \mathrm{Var}\frac{1}{\theta_1(\alpha)}$$

Hence, for sufficiently large $\mathrm{Var}[1/\theta_1(\alpha)]$, we get

$$\frac{\partial \mathrm{MRS}}{\partial p} < 0$$

which implies a decline in the output of the industry whose price has

risen and changes in real factor rewards which are opposite to those
suggested by the Stolper–Samuelson theorem. This completes the
example.

Now, suppose that we open the economy to trade in real equities.
Then, for our country, the relative price of a type-2 real equity is
given. Figure 7.6 describes the new stock market equilibrium; the
production point is E_{sp} and the portfolio point is E_{sc}. The slope of
the assets–budget line is q; the relative world price of type-2 real
equities. It can be seen that an increase in q will induce resource
movements toward the second industry, and increase the real reward
of the factor that is used more intensively in that industry. Hence, the
Stolper–Samuelson theorem holds with regard to changes in equity
prices. It does not hold with regard to commodity prices. For if, for
example, a commodity price goes up and equity prices do not change,
real rewards to factors of production in terms of equities do not change.

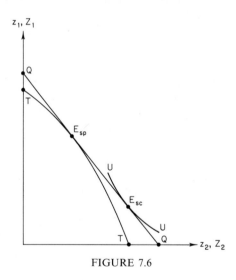

FIGURE 7.6

7.4   THE RYBCZYNSKI THEOREM

The Rybczynski theorem points out that if commodity prices are
kept constant but the endowment of some factor rises, the industry
using that factor relatively intensively expands—and the industry

using the other factor relatively intensively contracts. This theorem also fails to hold under conditions of uncertainty if there is no international trade in securities.

Consider Figure 7.4. Suppose *EE* stands for the wealth–portfolio line of the home country, which is derived from the assets–indifference curves. It is clear that the Rybczynski line need not coincide with the wealth–portfolio line. The increase in the endowment of the factor used more intensively by the second industry at unchanged real-equity prices would cause output changes indicated by points on the Rybczynski line. However, if real-equity prices are unchanged, demand for real equities would be indicated by points on the wealth–portfolio line, which is not an equilibrium situation. It is seen from Figure 7.4 that real-equity prices have to change, although the distribution of commodity prices is kept constant, in order for the local demand for real equities to match local supply. The diagram indicates that the relative price of type-2 real equities will decrease; in the new equilibrium, expected output of the second industry will be larger—but the expected output of the first industry need not decline.

Furthermore, from portfolio theory we know that the wealth effect on securities is not unambiguously positive, so the wealth–portfolio line need not be positively sloped. If demand for type-2 real equities responds negatively to an increase in wealth, the expected output of the second industry could decline.

When international trade in equities is allowed, a small open economy faces given real-equity prices. In this case an increase in the endowment of a factor of production will generate the Rybczynski effect because equity prices do not change Hence, in an uncertain world the Rybczynski theorem is saved if properly reformulated; namely, if what is kept constant is equity prices and not necessarily commodity prices. This is very clear if we remember that in an economy with stock markets, production decisions depend on equity prices and not on commodity prices.

7.5   THE HECKSCHER–OHLIN THEOREM

The Heckscher–Ohlin theorem links the pattern of trade to factor intensities and factor endowments. There are two definitions of relative factor abundance—the quantity and the value definitions. The quantity definition is based on relative factor endowments, while the value definition is based on relative factor prices. The Heckscher–Ohlin theorem under the quantity definition of relative factor abundance requires more stringent conditions than under the value definition of relative factor abundance. We concentrate, therefore, on the value version which states that a country exports the commodity which is relatively intensive in the factor whose relative reward prior to trade is lower than abroad.

That this theorem fails to hold under uncertainty, with or without international trade in equities, is clear from the fact that the pattern of trade may be state dependent (see Chapter 6); that is, a country may export one commodity in some states of nature, yet import this commodity in other states of nature.

Can the pattern of equity trade be linked to factor intensities and factor endowments? If we were assured that the posttrade relative equity prices lie between the pretrade relative equity prices of the country, then we could have provided an affirmative answer using the standard argument of the value version of the Heckscher–Ohlin theorem. The preceding condition on equity prices is satisfied if the pretrade preferences over securities prevail also in the posttrade situation. However, no such assurances exist. The opening of trade changes the distribution of commodity prices, which, in turn, changes the preferences over securities. The change in preferences may induce posttrade real-equity prices to lie outside the pretrade bounds.

REFERENCES

Ethier, W. (1974). Some of the theorems of international trade with many goods and factors, *Journal of International Economics* **4**, 199–206.
Jones, R. W., and Scheinkman, J. A. (1977). The relevance of the two-sector production model in trade theory, *Journal of Political Economy* **85**, 909–935.
Mundell, R. A. (1957). International trade and factor mobility, *American Economic Review* **47**, 327–335.

Chapter 8

Commercial Policy

The theory of commercial policy deals with both welfare and positive issues [Corden (1971, 1974)]. The welfare theory assesses the social benefits and losses from tariff systems. The positive theory is concerned with the direction and magnitude of resource reallocation effects under the influence of tariffs.

This chapter analyzes commercial policies in the presence of uncertainty. We analyze the general equilibrium effects of a tariff on the allocation of resources between the importable and exportable sectors, and welfare losses from tariffs. We apply the tools of analysis of protection in the presence of uncertainty only to tariffs; the effects of uncertainty on other commercial policies, such as production subsidies and quotas, can be similarly analyzed. We begin with a brief review of the traditional (deterministic) analysis of tariffs.

8.1 THE DETERMINISTIC MODEL

Assume that there are only two products in the economy—the exportable 1, and the importable 2. From the factor endowments of the economy and the two production functions, a production possibility curve, TT in Figure 8.1, can be derived. Assume that the country faces a given world price ratio (the small-country assumption) represented by the slope of BB in Figure 8.1. The point of tangency to the production possibility curve of a line with such a slope determines the production equilibrium point P.

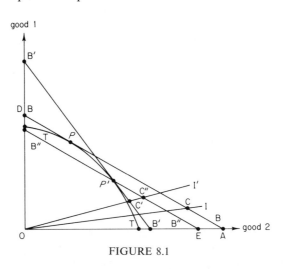

FIGURE 8.1

Assume that consumers are identical in tastes and endowments. Let $0I$ be the income–consumption line associated with the price ratio given by the slope of BB. Given production at P and the world price ratio, income is $0A$ in terms of good 2, or $0D$ in terms of good 1. Consumption equilibrium is at point C, where the income–consumption line $0I$ intersects BB.

Figure 8.1 shows that the production of good 1 exceeds the consumption of good 1, with the excess being exported, while the consumption of good 2 exceeds the production of good 2, with the excess being imported. The value of exports and the value of imports are equal at the given price ratio.

Now consider the imposition of an ad valorem tariff on imports. A tariff raises the domestic price of good 2 relative to that of good 1. The tariff–inclusive domestic price ratio is indicated by the slope of the line $B'B'$. The tariff thus leads to a production shift away from good 1 toward good 2; the new production point is P'. This is the *production effect* of the tariff. The tariff also leads to a movement from the income–consumption line $0I$ to the income–consumption line $0I'$. This is the *consumption effect* of the tariff. Assume that the tariff revenue is distributed back to consumers in a lump-sum fashion. The new consumption point must be at C'', where the posttariff income–consumption line $0I'$ intersects the new trade possibilities line $B''B''$, where $B''B''$ is determined by the world price ratio and the posttariff production point.[1] The lower level of income at world prices ($0E$ instead of $0A$) means that welfare losses are associated with the tariff.

8.2 PROTECTION UNDER UNCERTAINTY

We have seen that in the standard deterministic two-sector economy the imposition of a tariff induces a resource flow from the export to the import-competing industry if the external terms of trade do not change. This is the small-country case. It is also known that in the large-country case; that is, in the case in which the import (export) volume of a country influences its external terms of trade, an imposition of a tariff may induce a resource flow out of the import-competing industry and into the export industry. This is known as the Metzler paradox (Metzler, 1949). In the small-country case the imposition of the tariff necessarily reduces the internal terms of trade, because the external terms of trade do not change. Since domestic competitive resource allocation is governed by the internal terms of trade, the deterioration in the internal terms of trade that follows the tariff leads to an expansion of the import-competing industry and to a contraction of the export industry. Hence, the tariff is protective in this case. In the large-country case the imposition of a tariff may increase the external terms of trade at a rate which exceeds the rate of tariff, in which case the internal terms of trade will improve, thereby reversing the direction of resource flow. If this happens, the tariff is said to protect the export industry and not the import-competing industry.

We show in this section that in the presence of uncertainty a tariff need not provide protection to the import-competing industry even in the small-country case. The situation in which this may occur is one in which there is international trade in commodities but no international trade in securities. If there is international trade in securities, a tariff provides the conventional protection.

---

[1] If the tariff proceeds were not distributed back to consumers, the consumption point would have been C', which corresponds to the income line $B'B'$.

This paradox stems from the fact that in our model the allocation of factors of production is governed by equity prices, and it depends on commodity prices only to the extent that they influence equity prices. In the absence of international trade in securities, domestic equity prices are internally determined, since domestic risks are then fully borne by domestic residents. Now, the imposition of a tariff in a small country necessarily worsens the internal commodity terms of trade in every state of nature. However, its impact on relative equity prices, which determines the interindustry resource flow, depends on whether the tariff will shift the demand for *equities* toward the import competing sector or away from it. If tariff proceeds are not redistributed back to consumers, then the shift in the demand for equities can go either way, and we present an example in which demand shifts toward the equities of the exportable industry, in which case the tariff does not protect the import-competing industry. We also show that when tariff proceeds are redistributed back to consumers, a "small" tariff protects the import-competing industry if both goods are normal in consumption. This contrasts with the deterministic case in which the redistribution policy is not relevant for the protective effect of a tariff in the small-country case (it is though important for the large-country case).

We now turn to our model. Consider an ad valorem tariff on the second commodity, assuming that the second commodity is imported in every state of the world. The effects of the tariff on the allocation of resources between the two sectors differs according to whether international trade in securities takes place. We begin with the case of no international trade in securities, so that domestic residents bear all domestic risks.

A. No International Trade in Securities

The tariff-inclusive assets–indifference curves (which, along with the production possibilities curve, help determine the production of the economy) are given by

$$(8.1) \qquad Ev[(1 + t)p(\alpha); \theta_1(\alpha)z_1 + (1 + t)p(\alpha)\theta_2(\alpha)z_2 + T(\alpha, t)]$$
$$= \text{constant}$$

where t is the tariff rate (assumed to be state independent), and $T(\alpha, t)$ the state-α transfer payments. It tariff proceeds are redistributed back to consumers, $T(\alpha, t)$ equals tariff proceeds in state α, and it is equal to zero if tariff proceeds are not redistributed.

The tariff-inclusive marginal rate of substitution between real equity 2 and real equity 1, assuming that the individual perceives that the transfers he receives from tariff proceeds are not affected by changes in his portfolio, is given by

$$(8.2)\quad \mathrm{MRS}(z_1, z_2; t) \equiv \frac{\begin{array}{c} E(1 + t)p(\alpha)\theta_2(\alpha)v_i[(1 + t)p(\alpha); \\ \theta_1(\alpha)z_1 + (1 + t)p(\alpha)z_2 + T(\alpha, t)] \end{array}}{\begin{array}{c} E\theta_1(\alpha)v_i[(1 + t)p(\alpha); \theta_1(\alpha)z_1 \\ + (1 + t)p(\alpha)\theta_2(\alpha)z_2 + T(\alpha, t)] \end{array}}$$

Let us start with a discussion of the case in which tariff proceeds are not distributed back to consumers; that is, the government is using the revenue from tariffs in order to purchase commodities which do not influence consumer behavior or pay them out to foreigners.[2] Remember that in the small-country deterministic model a tariff protects the import competing industry regardless of whether tariff proceeds are redistributed. In the present case,

$$(8.3)\qquad T(\alpha, t) = 0 \qquad \text{for all } t \qquad \text{and} \qquad \alpha = 1, 2, \ldots, S$$

From (8.2) and (8.3) it is readily verified that a change in the tariff rate twists the assets–indifference curves at every point (z_1, z_2), and changes the marginal rate of substitution between real equities 2 and 1. This results from the fact that the tariff changes the mean as well as higher moments (such as the variance) of the distribution of the relative internal price of good 2.

In Figure 8.2, point E_s^0 denotes the pretariff stock market equilibrium in which the pretariff assets–indifference curve $U_0 U_0$ is tangent to the production possibilities curve TT. If the posttariff assets–indifference curve, which passes through the initial point E_s^0, is steeper than $U_0 U_0$, like $U_1 U_1$, the new equilibrium must be at a point on TT to the right of E_s^0; that is, resources are moving away from sector 1 and into the import-competing sector, sector 2, which is the standard case. If the posttariff assets–indifference curve which passes through E_s^0 is flatter than $U_0 U_0$, like $U_2 U_2$, the new equilibrium must be at a point on TT to the left of E_s^0; that is, resources are moving away from the importable goods sector and into the exportable goods sector. In the second case, a tariff does not protect the import-competing sector, contrary to the deterministic case. The following is an example in

---

[2] The first case occurs if, for example, the government uses tariff proceeds to provide public services, and the utility function is additively separable in private and public goods.

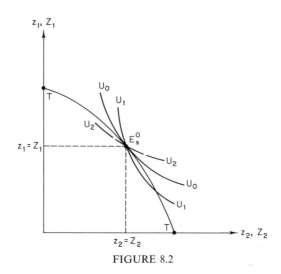

FIGURE 8.2

which this paradoxical result occurs. This is essentially the same as Example 7.2 which shows that the Stolper–Samuelson theorem does not hold.

EXAMPLE 8.1   Let the utility function be

$$u = \log(c_2 + \log c_1)$$

This yields the indirect utility function

$$v = \log\left\{\frac{I}{(1 + t)p} - 1 + \log[(1 + t)p]\right\}$$

where I stands for the consumer's disposable income. This implies [using (8.2) and (8.3)]

$$\text{MRS}(z_1, z_2; t) \equiv \frac{E[\theta_1(\alpha)(1 + t)^{-1}p(\alpha)^{-1}z_1 + \theta_2(\alpha)z_2 - 1 + \log(1 + t)p(\alpha)]^{-1}\theta_2(\alpha)}{E[\theta_1(\alpha)(1 + t)^{-1}p(\alpha)^{-1}z_1 + \theta_2(\alpha)z_2 - 1 + \log(1 + t)p(\alpha)]^{-1}\theta_1(\alpha)(1 + t)^{-1}p(\alpha)^{-1}}$$

Assume now that $\theta_2(\alpha) = 1$, $\theta_1(\alpha) > 1$, for all α, $p(\alpha) = 1$ for all α, and that at the initial equilibrium

$$t = 0$$

$$z_1 = z_2 = 1$$

These initial conditions imply that commodity 1 is exported in all states, since initially $c_1 = p = 1 < \theta_1(\alpha)z_1 = \theta_1(\alpha)$. The stockholders' choice of these real equity holdings can be assured by an appropriate choice of production technologies and factor endowments. Then, the derivative of MRS with respect to t, evaluated at the initial equilibrium, is

$$\frac{\partial \, \text{MRS}(z_1, z_2; 0)}{\partial t} = E \frac{1}{\theta_1(\alpha)} - \left[E\left(\frac{1}{\theta_1(\alpha)}\right)^2 - \left(E \frac{1}{\theta_1(\alpha)}\right)^2 \right]$$

$$= E\left[\frac{1}{\theta_1(\alpha)}\right] - \text{Var}\left[\frac{1}{\theta_1(\alpha)}\right]$$

Hence, for sufficiently large $\text{Var}[1/\theta_1(\alpha)]$, we get

$$\frac{\partial \, \text{MRS}(z_1, z_2; 0)}{\partial t} < 0$$

This implies that, for a "small" tariff, $U_2 U_2$ in Figure 8.2 is the post-tariff assets–indifference curve. Therefore, the imposition of the tariff leads to a contraction of the imports-competing industry and an expansion of the export industry.

In the absence of uncertainty, the variance of $1/\theta_1(\alpha)$ is zero and the paradoxical result does not arise. In the presence of uncertainty, the paradoxical result can arise because of the negative effect that an increase in t has on the demand for type-2 real equities, holding their returns constant. This can be seen as follows. Write the indirect utility function as

$$v = \log\{\theta_1(\alpha)(1 + t)^{-1}z_1 + z_2 - 1 + B(t)\}$$

where $B(t) = \log(1 + t)$. It can be shown that an increase in B reduces the demand for type-2 real equities. Now, an increase in the tariff rate has two effects. It increases B, resulting in a decline in the demand for type-2 real equities, and increases the return on type-2 real equities, resulting in an increase in its demand. The first effect, which is a negative income-type effect, dominates in this case when $\text{Var}[1/\theta_1(\alpha)]$ is large enough. This completes the example.

Consider now the case in which tariff proceeds are redistributed back to consumers. In this case, state-α transfers (that is, the tariff rate times the value of imports) are implicitly given by

$$(8.4) \quad T(\alpha, t) = tp(\alpha)\{c_2[(1 + t)p(\alpha); \theta_1(\alpha)z_1 + (1 + t)$$
$$\times \, \theta_2(\alpha)p(\alpha)z_2 + T(\alpha, t)] - \theta_2(\alpha)Z_2[q(t)]\}$$

where $c_2(\cdot)$ is the second commodity demand function, and $q(t)$ is the equilibrium relative price of type-2 real equity, which is a function of the tariff rate. Notice that from (8.4), we get

(8.5) $T(\alpha, 0) = 0$

$$\frac{\partial T(\alpha, 0)}{\partial t} = p(\alpha)\{c_2[p(\alpha); \theta_1(\alpha)z_1 + \theta_2(\alpha)p(\alpha)z_2]$$

$$- \theta_2(\alpha)Z_2[q(0)]\}$$

That is, a zero tariff rate obviously must give rise to a zero amount of tariff proceeds, and the rate of change in the tariff proceeds for a small tariff is equal to imports evaluated at world prices.

We show now that if both goods are normal, the paradoxical result cannot appear in the case of a small tariff. In order to see this, differentiate (8.2) with respect to t and evaluate it at $t = 0$ using (8.5) to obtain

$$\frac{\partial \, \mathrm{MRS}(z_1, z_2; 0)}{\partial t} = \frac{1}{Ev_1(\alpha)\theta_1(\alpha)} \{Ev_1(\alpha)p(\alpha)\theta_2(\alpha)$$

$$+ Ev_{1p}(\alpha)[p(\alpha)]^2\theta_2(\alpha)$$

$$+ Ev_{11}(\alpha)[p(\alpha)]^2c_2(\alpha)\theta_2(\alpha)$$

$$- \mathrm{MRS}(z_1, z_2; 0)[Ev_{1p}(\alpha)p(\alpha)\theta_1(\alpha)$$

$$+ Ev_{11}(\alpha)p(\alpha)c_2(\alpha)\theta_1(\alpha)]\}$$

where v_{1p} is the derivative of v_1 with respect to its first argument.
Now,

$$v_{1p} = v_{p1} = \frac{\partial(-v_1c_2)}{\partial I} = -v_{11}c_2 - v_1c_{21}$$

where $c_{21} = \partial c_2/\partial I$ and $pc_{21} = 1 - c_{11}$. Substituting these relationships in the above expression, we get

(8.6) $\dfrac{\partial \, \mathrm{MRS}(z_1, z_2; 0)}{\partial t} = \dfrac{1}{Ev_1(\alpha)\theta_1(\alpha)} \{Ev_1(\alpha)p(\alpha)\theta_2(\alpha)c_{11}(\alpha)$

$$+ \mathrm{MRS}(z_1, z_2;0)Ev_1(\alpha)\theta_1(\alpha)p(\alpha)c_{21}(\alpha)\}$$

If both goods are normal, the marginal propensities to spend on the goods are positive and the expression in (8.6) is positive. This means that for normal goods a small tariff will twist the assets–indifference curves in Figure 8.2 so as to make them steeper, as from U_0U_0 to U_1U_1, and thus provide protection to the importable goods sector.

At this point it is useful to reconsider the relationship between the Stolper–Samuelson theorem and the protective effect of a tariff. In the deterministic Heckscher–Ohlin model, it is customary to use the Stolper–Samuelson theorem in order to show that tariff protection increases the real income of the factor that is used relatively intensively in the import-competing industry, and that it reduces the real income of the other factor. The argument is as follows. According to the Stolper–Samuelson theorem, an increase in the relative price of a good induces a resource movement into the industry whose relative price increased and away from the other industry. This resource flow increases the real income of the factor that is used more intensively in the expanding industry and reduces the real income of the other factor. Now, a tariff raises the domestic relative price of importables and thus simulates the Stolper–Samuelson effect.

However, in Chapter 7 we provided an example (Example 7.2) in which, in the case of no international trade in equities, an increase in the price of a good leads to a flow of resources away from the industry that produces that good, causing a decline in the real income of the factor used relatively intensively in that industry and an increase in the real income of the other factor. This example had one normal and one neutral good, so that according to (8.6) if we were to use the data of the example in order to evaluate the effect of a tariff with tariff revenue redistribution, we would have found that the tariff is protective in the sense that it increases the output of the import-competing industry and the real income of the factor used relatively intensively in that industry. If, however, tariff proceeds are not redistributed, the effect of a tariff is in line with the Stolper–Samuelson effect. We see, therefore, that under uncertainty the Stolper–Samuelson effect is not necessarily the same as the tariff effect. This divergence stems from the fact that in the case of a tariff with revenue transfers, the revenue transfers generate income effects on the demand for assets which are absent in the case of an exogenous price change. These income effects are not important for the determination of the direction of resource flows in the deterministic model, but they are important under uncertainty. This is why the Stolper–Samuelson and the tariff effects coincide in the deterministic model but not in our stochastic model.

Finally, observe that an equity subsidy, that is, a subsidy given to an industry at the *financing stage*, will unambiguously induce the expansion of that industry. In Figure 8.3 we reconstruct the initial equilibrium shown in Figure 8.2, the real equity–price ratio being q. A subsidy to sales of real equity 2 decreases to q' the relative price of real equity 2 to investors, and drives a wedge between that relative price and the marginal rate of transformation q'', leading to a new equilibrium E_s'. Thus, resources will move away from sector 1 and into sector 2 regardless of the subsidy's size.

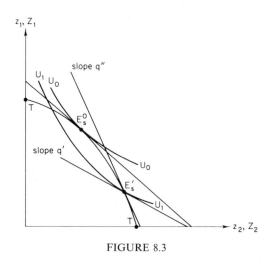

FIGURE 8.3

B.   International Trade in Securities

Consider the case in which the economy trades with the outside world in both commodities and securities. By the small-country assumption, without a tariff, commodity prices and security prices are given to the home country. A tariff raises the local price of the importable goods; but how does a tariff affect the stock market value of the importable-goods industry?

Since a tariff at a rate of $100t$ percent increases the price of the second commodity by $100t$ percent in every state of the world, it increases by $100t$ percent the return on each unit of type-2 real equities. It is therefore clear that if the price of type-2 real equities does not change, it will become very attractive to foreign and local investors— who will shift their portfolios from foreign type-2 real equities to the local ones. This will result in a $100t$ percent increase in the price of local type-2 real equities in order to eliminate profitable arbitrage. The local type-2 real equity provides a return of $(1 + t)\theta_2(\alpha)p(\alpha)$ in every state α, while the foreign type-2 real equity provides a return of $\theta_2(\alpha)p(\alpha)$ in state α. Hence, one unit of local type-2 real equity is now equivalent to $(1 + t)$ units of foreign type-2 real equities.

This means that the price of local type-2 real equities has increased from q to $(1 + t)q$. Thus, following a tariff, resources move away from the exportable-goods industry and into the importable-goods industry.

8.3 WELFARE LOSSES FROM TARIFFS

In the standard deterministic model it does not matter whether tariffs are specific or ad valorem since every specific tariff has an ad valorem equivalent. In the case of uncertainty, and in particular in our model, it is important whether the tariff is specific or ad valorem. A state-independent ad valorem tariff has a specific tariff equivalent which is state dependent, and conversely, a state-independent specific tariff has a state-dependent ad valorem tariff equivalent. But a state-independent ad valorem tariff does not change the structure of returns, whereas a state-independent specific tariff, or its state-dependent ad valorem equivalent, change the patterns of returns. This difference is important and we will expand on it at a later stage. (Observe also that in a deterministic inflationary situation, the two tariffs are not equivalent unless the specific tariff is indexed to the price level.)

We now turn to an analysis of the welfare implications of commodity trade taxes under uncertainty. We continue to assume that the second commodity is imported in every state of the world. Let us start by considering the case in which international trade in securities does not take place.

In Figure 8.4, point $E_s^{\,0}$ denotes the pretariff stock market equilibrium at which the community reaches an expected utility level $U_0 U_0$.

Suppose that an ad valorem tariff is imposed on imports, twisting the assets–indifference curves. For the present purpose, it is irrelevant whether the tariff rate is state dependent. In Figure 8.4, the posttariff production and portfolio point is E_s', at which the economy reaches an expected utility level $U'U'$. In Figure 8.5, the posttariff consumption equilibrium point is $E_t'(\alpha)$, at which the indifference curve $u'(\alpha)u'(\alpha)$ is tangent to $B'(\alpha)B'(\alpha)$. The slope of $B'(\alpha)B'(\alpha)$ is $(1 + t)p(\alpha)$, where t is the tariff rate. Given the posttariff production point $P'(\alpha)$ and the

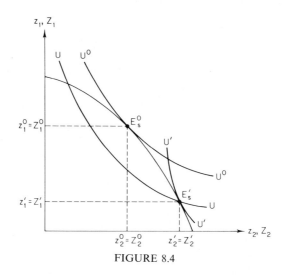

FIGURE 8.4

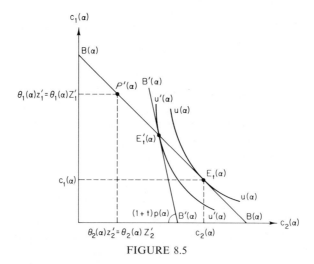

FIGURE 8.5

amount of tariff revenue returned to consumers, the consumers' budget line is $B'(\alpha)B'(\alpha)$. $B(\alpha)B(\alpha)$ is the trade possibilities line in state α, the slope of which is $p(\alpha)$. The posttariff consumption point $E_t'(\alpha)$ is at the point of intersection of $B(\alpha)B(\alpha)$ and $B'(\alpha)B'(\alpha)$. Observe that the second commodity is imported.

Welfare losses from the tariff are demonstrated through a backward movement from the posttariff equilibrium to the pretariff equilibrium

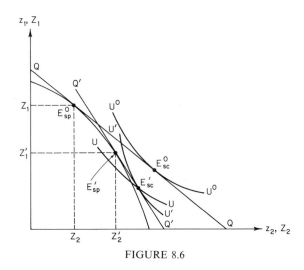

FIGURE 8.6

in two separate steps. In the first step, the production and portfolio composition of the economy do not change from the posttariff equilibrium, but the tariff is removed; this will be shown to involve a welfare gain. In the second step, the economy adjusts its production and portfolio; this will be shown to involve an additional welfare gain. The analysis is carried out under the assumption that foreign commodity prices do not change.

First, consider the pretariff assets–indifference curve that passes through E_s' in Figure 8.4, which is denoted by UU. Given that production and portfolio composition, without a tariff the economy consumes at point $E_t(\alpha)$, which lies on a higher indifference curve $u(\alpha)u(\alpha)$ in every state of the world (Figure 8.5). Therefore, the assets–indifference curve UU indicates a higher level of expected utility than does $U'U'$. Hence, the first step toward free trade involves a welfare gain.

Second, consider the free-trade equilibrium E_s^0 in Figure 8.4, in which the pretariff assets–indifference curve U^0U^0 is tangent to the production possibilities curve. Obviously, U^0U^0 indicates a higher level of expected utility than does UU. Hence, the second step toward free trade involves an additional welfare gain.

Now consider the case in which the economy trades with the outside world in both commodities and securities. The new pretariff stock market equilibrium is depicted in Figure 8.6.[3] E_{sp}^0 is the production point, E_{sc}^0 is the portfolio point, and U^0U^0 indicates the pretariff

---

[3] We assume, although it is not necessary, that type-2 securities are imported.

expected utility level. The slope of the QQ line is q, the price of a type-2 real equity in terms of a type-1 real equity.

As already explained, a tariff at a rate of $100t$ percent, which increases the return on each unit of type-2 real equity by the same percentage, will result in a $100t$ percent increase in the price of a local type-2 real equity.[4] This means that the price of local type-2 real equities is now $(1 + t)q$. On the horizontal axis, we measure type-2 real equities in local terms. This means that if the economy imports, say, 100 units of type-2 equities in local terms, it imports in fact $100(1 + t)$ units of foreign type-2 equities.

We can now analyze the effect of a tariff by means of Figure 8.6. A tariff generates two effects. First, the assets–budget line changes its slope from q to $(1 + t)q$ and becomes $Q'Q'$ instead of QQ. The new production point is now E'_{sp}. Second, the tariff generates a new indifference field, as already explained. $U'U'$ is the highest tariff-inclusive assets–indifference curve which passes through E'_{sc}, the posttariff portfolio equilibrium point. UU is the pretariff assets–indifference curve which passes through E'_{sc}.

It is clear that in the situation described in Figure 8.6, the tariff reduces welfare—because $U'U'$ represents a lower expected utility level than does UU, due to the argument based on Figure 8.5, and the economy will move to a still higher assets–indifference curve U^0U^0 in the free-trade situation. However, this need not be the case. Using the same notation, an alternative situation is depicted in Figure 8.7. Here we see that the economy can choose a portfolio, represented by the

---

[4] Note that the tariff actually generates a new type of asset. But in the simple case discussed above, the returns on the new asset are a linear combination (with all the weight on the type-2 foreign real equity) of the returns of the pretariff existing assets. More generally, when the tariff rate is state dependent, the new asset may provide returns which either are or are not a linear combination of the returns of the pretariff existing assets. In the former case, the so-called "spanning condition" is satisfied [see, in particular, Ekern and Wilson (1974)], and the value of the new security will be a linear combination of the values of the existing securities. But in the second case, the value of the new security cannot be derived from the prices of the pretariff existing securities. Whenever the spanning condition is not satisfied, it is not possible to prove generally that a tariff reduces welfare, because the new type of security generated by the tariff has a positive welfare effect due to its increase of the attainable consumption set. Observe also that this problem does not exist when there is no international trade in securities; in this case, the new type of asset generated by the tariff *replaces* the old asset, and our proof of welfare loss applies irrespective of whether the spanning condition is satisfied. These remarks are relevant in particular for comparisons of specific with ad valorem tariffs, but we do not consider this issue here.

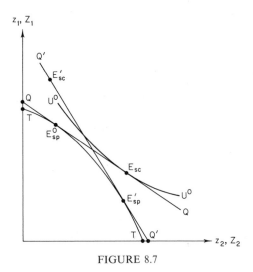

FIGURE 8.7

point E'_{sc}, which was not feasible in the pretariff situation. Hence, it cannot be seen from the geometrical analysis that the tariff-inclusive assets–indifference curve which passes through E'_{sc} represents a lower expected utility level than does $U^0 U^0$. Nevertheless, we now show by means of simple calculus that a tariff necessarily reduces welfare in this case—the case of an ad valorem state-independent tariff rate in the presence of international trade in goods and securities.

Let $c^t(\alpha)$ and $c(\alpha)$ be the optimal two-dimensional consumption bundles, corresponding respectively to the posttariff and pretariff situations. From concavity of the ordinary utility function $u(\cdot)$, we have

$$(8.7) \quad \sum_{\alpha=1}^{s} \pi(\alpha) u[c^t(\alpha)] < \sum_{\alpha=1}^{s} \pi(\alpha) u[c(\alpha)]$$

$$+ \sum_{\alpha=1}^{s} \pi(\alpha) \, \nabla u[c(\alpha)][c^t(\alpha) - c(\alpha)]$$

where $\pi(\alpha)$ is the subjective probability of state α, $\nabla u[\cdot]$ is the gradient vector [the vector of partial derivatives of $u(\cdot)$], and the last term on the right-hand side of (8.7) the inner product of the two vectors.

From the standard consumer first-order conditions, we know that

$$\nabla u[c(\alpha)] = v_1(\alpha)[1, p(\alpha)]$$

where $v_1(\alpha)$ is the marginal utility of income in the pretariff situation in state α. Hence,

$$(8.8) \quad \sum_{\alpha=1}^{S} \pi(\alpha) \nabla u[c(\alpha)][c^t(\alpha) - c(\alpha)]$$

$$= \sum_{\alpha=1}^{S} \pi(\alpha) v_i(\alpha)[c_1{}^t(\alpha) + p(\alpha)c_2{}^t(\alpha) - c_1(\alpha) - p(\alpha)c_2(\alpha)]$$

Let $(z_1{}^t, z_2{}^t)$ and (z_1, z_2) be the posttariff and pretariff optimal portfolios. Then, we have from the consumer budget constraint

$$(8.9) \qquad c_1(\alpha) + p(\alpha)c_2(\alpha) = \theta_1(\alpha)z_1 + \theta_2(\alpha)p(\alpha)z_2$$

and

$$(8.10) \quad c_1{}^t(\alpha) + (1 + t)p(\alpha)c_2{}^t(\alpha) = \theta_1(\alpha)z_1{}^t + \theta_2(\alpha)(1 + t)p(\alpha)z_2{}^t$$
$$+ tp(\alpha)[c_2{}^t(\alpha) - \theta_2(\alpha)Z_2{}^t]$$

where $Z_2{}^t$ is the posttariff production of local type-2 real equities, and the last term on the right-hand side of (8.10) is the tariff proceeds. $z_2{}^t$ is expressed in terms of local type-2 real equities.[5]
   Substituting (8.9) and (8.10) into (8.8), we get

$$(8.11) \quad \sum_{\alpha=1}^{S} \pi(\alpha) \nabla u[c(\alpha)][c^t(\alpha) - c(\alpha)]$$

$$= \sum_{\alpha=1}^{S} \pi(\alpha) v_i(\alpha)[\theta_1(\alpha)z_1{}^t + \theta_2(\alpha)p(\alpha)z_2{}^t$$

$$- \theta_1(\alpha)z_1 - \theta_2(\alpha)p(\alpha)z_2 + tp(\alpha)\theta_2(\alpha)(z_2{}^t - Z_2{}^t)]$$

From the assets–budget constraint, we have

$$(8.12) \qquad\qquad z_1{}^t + (1 + t)qz_2{}^t = Z_1{}^t + (1 + t)qZ_2{}^t$$

$$(8.13) \qquad\qquad z_1 + qz_2 = Z_1 + qZ_2$$

where Z_j is the pretariff production of type-j real equities. Substituting (8.12) and (8.13) into (8.11), and making use of the first-order condition for the optimal portfolio choice, (5.24), we obtain

$$(8.14) \quad \sum_{\alpha=1}^{S} \pi(\alpha) \nabla u[c(\alpha)][c^t(\alpha) - c(\alpha)]$$

$$= (Z_1{}^t + qZ_2{}^t - Z_1 - qZ_2) \sum_{\alpha=1}^{S} \pi(\alpha)v_i(\alpha)\theta_1(\alpha)$$

[5] Imports of foreign type-2 real equities (if they are imported) are $(z_2{}^t - Z_2{}^t)(1 + t)$.

From net market value maximization (the tangency of the QQ and the $Q'Q'$ curves to TT in Figure 8.5), we have

$$Z_1{}^t + qZ_2{}^t - Z_1 - qZ_2 < 0$$

Therefore, the right-hand side of (8.14) is negative, which, together with (8.7), implies

$$\sum_{\alpha=1}^{S} \pi(\alpha)u[c^t(\alpha)] < \sum_{\alpha=1}^{S} \pi(\alpha)u[c(\alpha)]$$

This proves that the posttariff expected utility level is smaller than the pretariff expected utility level.

In Appendix A, it is shown that the following represents the change in expected utility resulting from a small tariff:

$$(8.15) \quad \frac{t^2}{2} E \left\{ v_I(\alpha)p(\alpha)[c_{2p}^c(\alpha)p(\alpha) - \theta_2(\alpha)qZ_2'(q)] \right.$$

$$\left. + v_{II}(\alpha)[p(\alpha)\theta_2(\alpha) - \theta_1(\alpha)q]^2 \left[\frac{dz_2}{dt} - Z_2(q) \right]^2 \right\}$$

where $c_{2p}^c(\alpha)$ is the pretariff own price effect of the compensated demand for c_2 in state α, which is negative; $Z_2'(q)$ the derivative of the general equilibrium supply function of type-2 real equities with respect to q, which is positive; $v_{II}(\alpha)$ the pretariff income derivative of the marginal utility of income in state α, which is negative due to the concavity of $u(\cdot)$; and dz_2/dt the derivative of the demand for type-2 real equities with respect to the tariff rate, evaluated at $t = 0$.

It is clear that (8.15) is negative, so that a tariff incurs a welfare loss. Also observe that in the certainty situation described by $\theta_1(\alpha) = \theta_2(\alpha) = 1$ and $p(\alpha) = q$, for all α, this expression reduces to

$$\frac{t^2}{2} v_I p^2 (c_{2p}^c - Z_2')$$

which is the conventional measure for welfare losses from tariffs. The first term in the parentheses (c_{2p}^c) represents the consumption effect, while the second term (Z_2') represents the production effect. In the present context we have, in addition to the consumption and production effect, a portfolio effect, which is represented by the second part of (8.15).

REFERENCES

Corden, W. M. (1971). "The Theory of Protection." Oxford Univ. Press, London and New York.
Corden, W. M. (1974). "Trade Policy and Economic Welfare." Oxford Univ. Press, London and New York.
Ekern, S., and Wilson, R. (1974). On the theory of the firm in an economy with incomplete markets, *Bell Journal of Economics and Management Science* **5**, 171–179.
Metzler, L. A. (1949). Tariffs, the terms of trade, and the distribution of national income, *Journal of Political Economy* **57**, 1–29.

Chapter 9

Gains from Trade

There are gains from international trade in a world of full certainty because trade enlarges the set of consumption opportunities of a country. This chapter shows that under conditions of uncertainty the same reason implies gains from trade for a small country even though we do not allow for complete risk-sharing arrangements.

We shall consider gains from two types of trade: in commodities and in securities. This we shall consider for both small and large countries as well as for situations in which commodity trade is restricted by tariffs. We shall see that the deterministic argument concerning gains from trade cannot be used in all these situations, but welfare gains from trade can still be proved in some of them.

9.1 GAINS FROM TRADE FOR
A SMALL COUNTRY

Let us start with the small-country case. We use the diagrammatic apparatus developed in Chapter 6 to demonstrate the presence of gains from international trade in commodities and securities. The analysis involves two stages: first, starting from complete autarky, international trade in commodities is introduced; second, the economy opens to international trade in securities.

The pretrade position of the country is represented in Figure 9.1 by point E_s^0 at which the assets–indifference curve U_0U_0 is tangent to the real-equity transformation curve TT. The autarkic position for the state of the world α is represented in Figure 9.2 by the production and consumption point $P^0(\alpha)$. The relative price of good 2 is endogenously determined within the country, and is given by the slope of the indifference curve $u_0(\alpha)u_0(\alpha)$ that passes through point $P^0(\alpha)$.

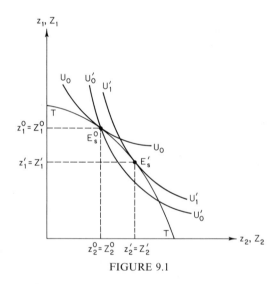

FIGURE 9.1

Now suppose that we open the economy to international trade in goods. Allowing for international trade in commodities at a relative price shown by the slope of the line $B'(\alpha)B'(\alpha)$, the home country could export $\theta_1(\alpha)Z_1^0 - c_1'(\alpha)$ units of good 1 to obtain $c_2'(\alpha) - \theta_2(\alpha)Z_2^0$ units of good 2 without changing the production composition, and thus improve its state-α welfare position to the level shown by the indifference curve $u_0'(\alpha)u_0'(\alpha)$. This gain in welfare in every state of the world, which necessarily implies an increase in the level of expected utility obtained from the original portfolio, is represented in Figure 9.1 by a new assets–indifference curve $U_0'U_0'$ which passes through the

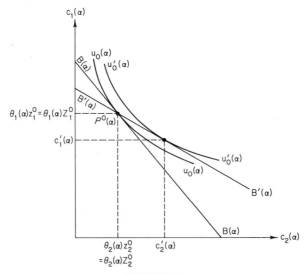

FIGURE 9.2

original production–portfolio point E_s^0. This curve is a member of a new map of assets–indifference curves denoted by primes.[1]

The highest achievable expected utility level is shown by the assets–indifference curve $U_1'U_1'$, and the new production–portfolio point which is common to this curve and to the real-equity transformation curve is E_s'.

The total gain from commodity trade can therefore be decomposed into

(1) the gain attributable to consuming at prices different from the original home prices—the movement from the assets–indifference curve U_0U_0 to the assets–indifference curve $U_0'U_0'$, and
(2) the gain attributable to the change in production and portfolio—the movement from the assets–indifference curve $U_0'U_0'$ to the assets–indifference curve $U_1'U_1'$.

[1] Note that for any portfolio (z_1, z_2) the slope of the new assets–indifference curve evaluated at this point would usually be different from the slope of the original assets–indifference curve, because the marginal rate of substitution between z_1 and z_2 is generally a function of the distribution of prices.

Observe now that so far we have not used the small-country assumption. This means that our argument about gains from commodity trade applies to both small and large countries, interpreting the slope of $B'(\alpha)B'(\alpha)$ as the postcommodity-trade state-α equilibrium relative commodity price.

Now let us return to the small-country case, and let the economy open to international trade in equities at a relative real-equity price q which is lower than the pretrade relative real-equity price. Commodity prices are assumed to remain the same; that is, in every state α the relative price of good 2 remains the same. In Figure 9.3 the presecurities-trade position of the country is represented by the point E_s' (reconstructed from Figure 9.1). Allowing for international trade in real equities, the production point moves from E_s' to E_{sp} (at E_{sp} the marginal rate of transformation equals q) and the portfolio point moves from E_s' to E_{sc}, thus improving the welfare position of the country to the level shown by the assets–indifference curve $U_2'U_2'$. A similar welfare improvement can be exhibited for a q larger than the initial one. Hence, international trade in securities at security prices different from the home prices in the presence of only trade in commodities necessarily improves welfare.

The result of this section implies that there are gains from international trade even if large uncertainties are involved. To see this, consider a small country which does not have any technological

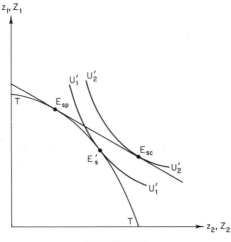

FIGURE 9.3

uncertainty; that is, $\theta_1(\alpha) = \theta_2(\alpha) = 1$ for all $\alpha = 1, \ldots, S$. Without international trade in goods and securities, this country faces certain commodity prices, and the composition of its consumption and production are state independent; in other words, the country lives in a standard world of full certainty. Now, suppose our country is opened to international trade in commodities with random foreign prices; our proposition states that the country will gain from international trade independently of how wildly foreign prices fluctuate. If, in addition, it opens to international trade in equities, it will experience additional welfare gains.

In Section 9.3 we shall discuss gains from restricted trade for a small country, and in Section 9.4 we shall discuss gains from trade for a large country.

9.2   AN IMPROVEMENT IN THE TERMS OF TRADE

A well-known proposition in the deterministic trade theory is that an improvement in the terms of trade of a country is always desirable. We shall now consider this premise under conditions of uncertainty.

Consider an improvement in the terms of trade in some state of the world. Two ex-post (state-α) free-trade situations—before and after the improvement has occurred—are shown in Figure 9.4 for a *given* portfolio (z_1, z_2).

It is seen that the improvement in the terms of trade shifts the budget line from $B(\alpha)B(\alpha)$ to $B'(\alpha)B'(\alpha)$, and results in a welfare gain— the movement from indifference curve $u(\alpha)u(\alpha)$ to indifference curve $u'(\alpha)u'(\alpha)$.

Assume, first, that international trade in equities does not take place. Figure 9.5 represents the expected utility change for this case. Point E_s is the stock market equilibrium point before the improvement in the terms of trade takes place. The indifference curve UU represents the expected utility level in this situation. Now suppose that the terms of trade improve in some states of nature. The gains in welfare in every state that were exhibited in Figure 9.4 imply a change in the assets– indifference field such that the new assets–indifference curve passing through the initial portfolio point E_s in Figure 9.5, $U''U''$, indicates a higher level of welfare than does the old assets–indifference curve passing through that portfolio point, UU. Hence, even if domestic

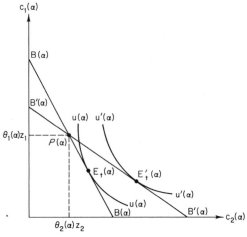

FIGURE 9.4

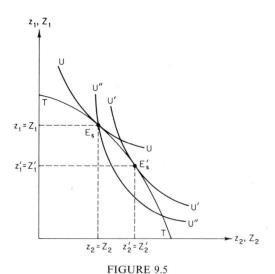

FIGURE 9.5

investors do not change their portfolio composition, they will be better off. But with the new terms of trade, E_s is no more the stock market equilibrium point. If equity prices do not change, then in the situation described in Figure 9.5 there will be an excess demand for type-2 real equities and their relative price will go up. Point E_s' describes the new equilibrium point.[2] Since $U'U'$, which passes through E_s', represents a higher expected utility than $U''U''$, the change in portfolio composition introduces an additional welfare gain.

When international trade in equities takes place, we cannot know a priori whether an improvement in the terms of commodity trade of the country leads to a welfare gain or loss, unless the terms of equity trade have not changed. If the terms of equity trade remain the same, then there is a welfare gain whose existence is easily established by the same method as in the case of no trade in securities (except that in the present case, production will not change and only the portfolio composition will change).

It is, however, very unlikely to have changes in relative commodity prices without changes in relative equity prices. The precise relationship between the movement in the terms of commodity and equity trade depends on the nature of the disturbance that triggered the change. For example, suppose that type-1 real equities are imported. If q falls (that is, there is a deterioration in the terms of equity trade), the loss from that change may more than offset the gain resulting from the improvement in the terms of commodity trade. As a result, the country may suffer a net loss.

9.3   GAINS FROM RESTRICTED TRADE

In this section we consider the gains from trade in the presence of a tariff at a fixed rate. The level of the tariff rate is arbitrary, call it t, but is kept constant throughout the analysis. The present discussion includes the special case $t = 0$; that is, unrestricted commodity trade.

We will show that:

(a)   If tariff proceeds are not redistributed back to consumers, then restricted trade in goods is preferred by consumers to complete autarky, and restricted trade in goods and unrestricted trade in securities is preferred by consumers to only restricted trade in goods.

(b)   If tariff proceeds are redistributed back to consumers, then restricted trade in goods is preferred by consumers to complete autarky.

---

[2] Point E_s' need not be to the right of E_s, as one can see from Example 7.2. The indifference curve $U''U''$ may happen to be flatter than UU at E_s. This, however, does not change the present welfare argument.

(c) If tariff proceeds are redistributed back to consumers, then restricted trade in goods and unrestricted security trade is preferred by consumers to complete autarky.

We were not able to show, in the presence of a redistribution of tariff proceeds, that trade in goods and securities is preferred by consumers to trade in only commodities. We believe that in this case trade in securities may be harmful, although we were not able to construct an example which demonstrates it. The reasons for our belief will be explained later.

A. Gains from Restricted Trade
when Tariff Proceeds are not Redistributed

For the case in which the tariffs are not redistributed back to consumers, the argument of Section 9.1, concerning the gains from trade, applies. The reason is that the results of Section 9.1 depend neither on the structure nor on the source of the structure of prices with which consumers are faced when trade opens up. In the present case consumers are faced with new commodity prices $(1 + t)p(\alpha)$, where $p(\alpha)$ is the world relative price of good 2.

B. Gains from Restricted Trade in Goods
when Tariff Proceeds are Redistributed

Let $c^t(\alpha)$ and $c(\alpha)$ be the equilibrium consumption bundles corresponding to the posttrade and pretrade situations. From the concavity of the utility function $u(\cdot)$, we have

$$(9.1) \qquad \sum_{\alpha=1}^{S} \pi(\alpha)u[c(\alpha)] - \sum_{\alpha=1}^{S} \pi(\alpha)u[c^t(\alpha)]$$

$$\leq \sum_{\alpha=1}^{S} \pi(\alpha)\, \nabla u[c^t(\alpha)][c(\alpha) - c^t(\alpha)]$$

where $\pi(\alpha)$ is the subjective probability of state α, $\nabla u(\cdot)$ the vector of partial derivatives of $u(\cdot)$, and the last term on the right-hand side of (9.1) the inner product of two vectors.

From standard consumer first-order conditions, we have

(9.2) $$\nabla u[c^t(\alpha)] = v_i(\alpha, t)[1, (1 + t)p(\alpha)]$$

where $v_i(\alpha, t)$ is the marginal utility of income in the posttrade situation in state α, and t is the tariff rate.

Substituting (9.2) into (9.1), we get

(9.3)
$$\sum_{\alpha=1}^{S} \pi(\alpha)u[c(\alpha)] - \sum_{\alpha=1}^{S} \pi(\alpha)u[c^t(\alpha)]$$

$$\leq \sum_{\alpha=1}^{S} \pi(\alpha)v_i(\alpha, t)[c_1(\alpha) + (1 + t)p(\alpha)c_2(\alpha)$$

$$- c_1{}^t(\alpha) - (1 + t)p(\alpha)c_2{}^t(\alpha)]$$

Let $(z_1{}^t, z_2{}^t)$ be the posttrade equilibrium portfolio vector, and (Z_1, Z_2) the pretrade equilibrium production (portfolio) vector.

From the consumer budget constraint,

(9.4) $$c_1{}^t(\alpha) + (1 + t)p(\alpha)c_2{}^t(\alpha) = \theta_1(\alpha)z_1{}^t + \theta_2(\alpha)(1 + t)p(\alpha)z_2{}^t$$
$$+ tp(\alpha)[c_2{}^t(\alpha) - \theta_2(\alpha)Z_2{}^t]$$

Assuming that commodity 2 is imported in all states,[3] the last term on the right-hand side of (9.4) is positive for all α, given $t > 0$.

Hence

(9.4a) $$c_1{}^t(\alpha) + (1 + t)p(\alpha)c_2{}^t(\alpha) > \theta_1(\alpha)z_1{}^t + \theta_2(\alpha)(1 + t)p(\alpha)z_2{}^t$$

No commodity trade implies

(9.5) $$c_i(\alpha) = \theta_i(\alpha)Z_i, \qquad i = 1, 2$$

while no international trade in securities after trade in commodities takes place implies

(9.6) $$z_i{}^t = Z_i{}^t = Z_i{}^t(q^t), \qquad i = 1, 2$$

where q^t is the posttrade domestic equilibrium relative price of real equities of type 2.

---

[3] This assumption is needed when restricted trade is compared to no trade, but is not needed when free trade (that is, $t = 0$) is compared to no trade.

Substituting (9.4a), (9.5) and (9.6) into (9.3), and using the first-order conditions for the portfolio composition problem [see (5.23)], we get

$$(9.7) \quad \sum_{\alpha=1}^{S} \pi(\alpha)u[c(\alpha)] - \sum_{\alpha=1}^{S} \pi(\alpha)u[c^t(\alpha)]$$

$$< \sum_{\alpha=1}^{S} \pi(\alpha)v_i(\alpha, t)[\theta_1(\alpha)Z_1$$

$$+ (1 + t)p(\alpha)\theta_2(\alpha)Z_2 - \theta_1(\alpha)Z_1{}^t - (1 + t)p(\alpha)\theta_2(\alpha)Z_2{}^t]$$

$$= (Z_1 + q^tZ_2 - Z_1{}^t - q^tZ_2{}^t) \sum_{\alpha=1}^{S} \pi(\alpha)v_i(\alpha, t)$$

$$\leq 0$$

The last inequality follows from net market value maximization, which implies $Z_1 + q^tZ_2 - Z_1{}^t - q^tZ_2{}^t \leq 0$. This completes the proof.

C. Gains from Restricted Trade in Goods and Unrestricted Trade in Securities when Tariff Proceeds are Redistributed

The proof is similar to that in Section B above except that superscript t now denotes the variables associated with trade in both goods and securities, and instead of (9.6), we have

$$(9.8) \qquad\qquad z_1{}^t + qz_2{}^t = Z_1{}^t + qZ_2{}^t$$

where q is the foreignly determined relative price of type-2 real equities.

We return now to the comparison between trade in goods and securities and trade in commodities only with a redistribution of tariff proceeds. When consumers make portfolio decisions, they do not take into account the impact of the portfolio composition on tariff revenue which affects their welfare level. Hence, they choose a suboptimal portfolio. This is true regardless of whether trade in securities takes place. Therefore, we here compare two second- (third-?) best situations, and we do not know which is preferred by consumers. The reader can check that the proof of Sections B and C cannot be used to prove superiority of trade in goods and securities over trade in goods only.

9.4 GAINS FROM TRADE FOR A LARGE COUNTRY

We explained in Section 9.1 that there are gains from commodity trade regardless of whether the country is small or large. Here, we discuss, therefore, only the problem of gains from security trade for a large country.

The potential loss from security trade for a large country lies in the possibility that as a result of trade in securities its terms of commodity trade will be adversely affected in at least some states of the world. We cannot exclude this possibility, neither could we prove that at least some countries have to gain from security trade.

It has been shown by Hart (1975) that in an economy with incomplete markets, the addition of a market may be harmful to all market participants. Since our model is a model with incomplete markets, although not exactly like the model used by Hart, his result suggests that there may well be circumstances under which free trade in commodities only will be preferred by all countries, or at least by some, to free trade in goods and securities.

REFERENCE

Hart, O. D. (1975). On the optimality of equilibrium when the market structure is incomplete, *Journal of Economic Theory* 11, 418–443.

Chapter 10

Efficient Intervention
in Financial Capital Markets

In this chapter we present three arguments for intervention in financial capital markets, and we analyze the optimal policy for each. In the first case, the country possesses monopoly power in security trade. In the second case, unremovable tariffs exist and their impact cannot be counteracted by means of intervention in commodity markets. In the third case, there exists a risk of default on foreign security holdings.

10.1 FIRST-BEST TAXATION OF EQUITIES

We present here an argument for equity taxation which is the counterpart of the optimal tariff argument. For this purpose we assume that our country has no monopoly power in commodity markets; that is, it faces given commodity prices in every state of the world. In addition, let us assume that there are no restrictions on trade in commodities. Should the government intervene in this situation in international capital flows? We want to show that the answer is negative if the country has no monopoly power in equity markets, and positive if it possesses such power.

First, consider the case in which the country is a price taker in equity markets. Its stock market equilibrium is described in Figure 10.1 (a reproduction of Figure 6.4); E_{sp} is the production point, and E_{sc} the portfolio composition point.

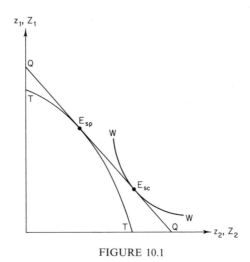

FIGURE 10.1

Suppose that taxes (subsidies) are imposed on the purchase of equities, and their proceeds are redistributed in the form of lump-sum transfers. Then, investors will be induced to choose a point on QQ which may differ from E_{sc}. Obviously, the investors' welfare level is reduced if they choose a point which differs from E_{sc}.

Now, suppose that taxes (subsidies) are imposed on the sale of equities, the proceeds of which are redistributed in a lump-sum fashion. Then the production point may move away from E_{sp}, but the terms at which equities are exchanged with the rest of the world will remain equal to the slope of QQ. Hence, the portfolio composition will have to be chosen from points on a line which is parallel to, and not higher than, QQ. Obviously, this means that welfare does not improve as a result of such policies, and it may even deteriorate.

It is also clear that there exists no combination of taxes (subsidies) on purchases and sales of equities which increases welfare. Hence, since taxes (subsidies) on equity imports (exports) can be considered as combinations of taxes on purchases and sales of equities, they also cannot lead to a welfare improvement.

Now consider the case in which the country has monopoly power in equity markets but not in commodity markets. This may happen if, for example, in the rest of the world there are no perfect substitutes for domestic real equities of type 1 (the exported equities), but there are perfect substitutes for domestic type-2 real equities. This happens when $\theta_2(\alpha)$ is the same at home and abroad, but $\theta_1(\alpha)$ has a different distribution at home and abroad. For the diagrammatical exposition it is then convenient to assume that local residents find it unattractive to hold foreign type-1 real equities. Let us represent that monopoly power by a foreign offer curve OO in Figure 10.2; an offer curve which is not a straight line.

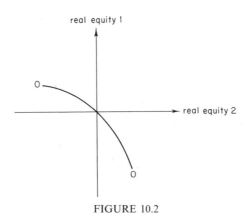

FIGURE 10.2

Following Baldwin's well-known exposition (Baldwin, 1948, 1952), we can superimpose the offer curve on the diagram in Figure 10.1 and slide its origin along the transformation curve in order to generate the portfolio possibilities locus—curve CC in Figure 10.3. CC is the collection of external points of the offer curve, the origin of which is slid along the transformation curve.

E, the point of tangency between an assets–indifference curve and CC, is the optimal portfolio composition. P is the production point which enables the attainment of E. QQ is the price line at which equities are exchanged with foreigners at the optimal allocation (optimal only from the point of view of the home country).

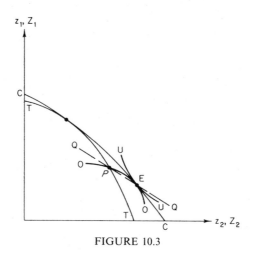

FIGURE 10.3

By construction, the slope of the transformation curve at P equals the slope of CC and UU at E, and they are larger than the slope of QQ. Therefore, a tax on imports of type-2 real equities at a rate which equals the difference between the above-mentioned slopes will support the optimal allocation.

10.2 A SECOND-BEST ARGUMENT
FOR EQUITY TAXATION

It is clear from previous discussions that in the absence of impediments to trade, a country which has no monopoly power in commodity and security markets will do best by maintaining a free-trade policy. Since tariffs are a fact of life, it is of interest to know what type of policies should be followed in their presence, provided they cannot be removed or neutralized indirectly by means of policies in commodity markets. This question was previously posed by Kemp (1966) and Jones (1967) in the context of international movements of physical capital (that is, international factor movements) in a deterministic world. They showed that in the presence of unremovable tariffs, and no possibility of intervening in commodity markets, the second-best policy generally calls for taxes or subsidies on earnings from domestic physical capital invested abroad or on foreign physical capital invested in the home country. This statement is valid even if the home country has no monopoly power in foreign trade.

In this section we analyze optimal intervention in financial capital flows in the presence of unremovable tariffs and the absence of feasible policy tools for intervening in commodity markets. We show that it is optimal to tax sales of equities by the (commodity) import-competing industry at the tariff rate, and that taxation of equity purchases may or may not be required. If required, it is not possible to determine what type of equity should be taxed (we continue to assume that there is no international movement of factors of production). The equity tax fully reverses the resource flow into the import-competing industry that was induced by the tariff, so that the production pattern is restored to that prevailing in a regime of free trade. We also show that in the case in which ordinal commodity preferences can be represented by a Cobb–Douglas utility function, it is optimal to abstain from intervention in equity purchases. The same result obtains for every utility function in the limiting case of full certainty. A discussion of this result in relation to the standard theory of international trade is provided at the end of this section.

Let us start the analysis by solving the optimal portfolio composition and the production point on the transformation curve. Then, we shall determine the structure of security prices which supports this allocation. From this price structure, we shall be able to derive the required taxes on sales and purchases of equities.

The planning problem of the portfolio composition and the choice of a production point can be represented as[1]

(10.1)   choose $z_1, z_2, Z_2 \geq 0$

to maximize

$Ev[\bar{p}(\alpha); \theta_1(\alpha)z_1 + \bar{p}(\alpha)\theta_2(\alpha)z_2 + T(\alpha, z_1, z_2, Z_2)]$

subject to

$z_1 + \bar{q}z_2 \leq \hat{Z}_1(Z_2) + \bar{q}Z_2$

where $\bar{p}(\alpha) = (1 + t)p(\alpha)$, $\bar{q} = (1 + t)q$, t is the tariff rate, and $\hat{Z}_1(Z_2)$ the functional form of the transformation curve. (See Chapter 8 for a

---

[1] Here we assume that tariff proceeds are redistributed back to consumers. If tariff proceeds are not redistributed, then it is easy to see that the second-best policy calls for no intervention in the security market. However, if tariff proceeds are used to supply public services and these influence the utility level, our qualitative results still hold.

discussion of the relationship between tariffs and the price structure.) As the reader can see, this formulation assumes that the second commodity is imported in every state of the world.

$T(\alpha, z_1, z_2, Z_2)$ describes the functional relationship between tariff proceeds—which are redistributed in a lump-sum fashion—portfolio composition, and the production pattern. $T(\cdot)$ is implicitly defined by

$$(10.2) \quad T(\alpha, z_1, z_2, Z_2) \equiv tp(\alpha)\{c_2[\bar{p}(\alpha); \theta_1(\alpha)z_1 + \bar{p}(\alpha)\theta_2(\alpha)z_1$$
$$+ T(\alpha, z_1, z_2, Z_2)] - \theta_2(\alpha)Z_2\}$$

From (10.2), we obtain

$$(10.3a) \qquad \frac{\partial T}{\partial z_1}(\alpha) = \frac{tp(\alpha)\theta_1(\alpha)c_{2I}(\alpha)}{1 - tp(\alpha)c_{2I}(\alpha)}$$

$$(10.3b) \qquad \frac{\partial T}{\partial z_2}(\alpha) = \frac{tp(\alpha)\bar{p}(\alpha)\theta_2(\alpha)c_{2I}(\alpha)}{1 - tp(\alpha)c_{2I}(\alpha)}$$

$$(10.3c) \qquad \frac{\partial T}{\partial Z_2}(\alpha) = -\frac{tp(\alpha)\theta_2(\alpha)}{1 - tp(\alpha)c_{2I}(\alpha)}$$

c_{2I} is the derivative of c_2 with respect to income. Hence, assuming that both goods are normal and that the tariff rate does not exceed 100 percent, we have

$$\frac{\partial T}{\partial z_i}(\alpha) > 0, \qquad i = 1, 2,$$

and

$$\frac{\partial T}{\partial Z_2}(\alpha) < 0$$

For notational convenience, we have suppressed all arguments in the functions except for the state of the world. This procedure will be followed throughout the present discussion.

Using μ as the Lagrangian multiplier, the first-order conditions for an interior solution of problem (10.1) are

$$(10.4a) \qquad Ev_I(\alpha)\left[\theta_1(\alpha) + \frac{\partial T}{\partial z_1}(\alpha)\right] - \mu = 0$$

$$(10.4b) \qquad Ev_I(\alpha)\left[\bar{p}(\alpha)\theta_2(\alpha) + \frac{\partial T}{\partial z_2}(\alpha)\right] - \mu\bar{q} = 0$$

(10.4c)
$$Ev_1(\alpha) \frac{\partial T}{\partial Z_2}(\alpha) + \mu(\bar{q} + \hat{Z}_1') = 0$$

where $\hat{Z}_1' = d\hat{Z}_1/dZ_2$ is the negative value of the marginal rate of transformation.

Producers choose a production point at which the marginal rate of transformation equals the relative real-equity price faced by them; that is, they consider the relative selling price of real equities. Thus, without tariffs and other interventions, production will take place at Z_2^0 such that

(10.5a)
$$q = -\hat{Z}_1'(Z_2^0)$$

With the tariff and no intervention in capital markets, they will choose Z_2^t such that

(10.5b)
$$q < \bar{q} = -\hat{Z}_1'(Z_2^t)$$

Since the transformation curve is concave, (10.5a) and (10.5b) imply

$$Z_2^0 < Z_2^t$$

Now, letting Z_2^{0p} stand for Z_2 which solves (10.1), (10.4c) implies

(10.5c)
$$\bar{q} + \frac{1}{\mu} Ev_1(\alpha) \frac{\partial T}{\partial Z_2}(\alpha) = -\hat{Z}_1'(Z_2^{0p})$$

Hence, since the second term on the left-hand side of (10.5c) is negative, (10.5b) and (10.5c) imply

$$Z^{0p} < Z_2^t$$

The tariff protects the second industry, inducing it to attract more resources than it would have attracted without the tariff. In this case, optimal intervention in capital markets requires that a tax be imposed on sales of type-2 real equities in order to discourage the overexpansion of that industry. The tax per equity should be

(10.6)
$$\tau = -\frac{1}{\mu} Ev_1(\alpha) \frac{\partial T}{\partial Z_2}(\alpha)$$

in terms of type-2 real equities, as one can see from (10.5c).

If $\tau < tq$, the equity tax only partially reverses the resource flow induced by the tariff; if $\tau > tq$, the equity tax overcompensates for the resource flow induced by the tariff. We now show that $\tau = tq$, which means that the optimal equity tax just offsets the impact of the tariff on the pattern of production, implying

$$Z_2^{0p} = Z_2^{0}$$

In order to prove that $\tau = tq$, we substitute (10.4b), (10.3b), and (10.3c) into (10.6) to obtain

$$\tau = -\bar{q} \frac{Ev_1(\alpha) \, \partial T(\alpha)/\partial Z_2}{Ev_1(\alpha)[\bar{p}(\alpha)\theta_2(\alpha) + (\partial T(\alpha)/\partial z_2)]}$$

$$= tq \frac{Ev_1(\alpha)\bar{p}(\alpha)\theta_2(\alpha)[1 - tp(\alpha)c_{21}(\alpha)]^{-1}}{Ev_1(\alpha)\bar{p}(\alpha)\theta_2(\alpha)[1 - tp(\alpha)c_{21}(\alpha)]^{-1}}$$

$$= tq$$

Now let us see the implications of an optimal portfolio composition. From (10.4a) and (10.4b), using (10.3a) and (10.3b), we obtain

(10.7)
$$\bar{q} = \frac{Ev_1(\alpha)\bar{p}(\alpha)\theta_2(\alpha)[1 - tp(\alpha)c_{21}(\alpha)]^{-1}}{Ev_1(\alpha)\theta_1(\alpha)[1 - tp(\alpha)c_{21}(\alpha)]^{-1}}$$

However, if $\tilde{q}$ is the relative real-equity price for investors, then an investor who considers the redistributed tariff proceeds as lump-sum transfers will choose a portfolio composition which equates his marginal rate of substitution between z_2 and z_1 to $\tilde{q}$. Hence, his portfolio choice satisfies

(10.8)
$$\tilde{q} = \frac{Ev_1(\alpha)\bar{p}(\alpha)\theta_2(\alpha)}{Ev_1(\alpha)\theta_1(\alpha)}$$

In general, the right-hand side of (10.8) may be larger than, equal to, or smaller than the right-hand side of (10.7), both evaluated at the optimal allocation. If it is larger, then the optimal policy calls for a tax on the purchase of type-2 real equities. If it is smaller, the optimal policy calls for a subsidy on the purchase of type-2 real equities.

Now consider a special case in which commodity preferences can be represented by a Cobb–Douglas utility function

(10.9)
$$u(c_1, c_2) = (c_1^{1-\beta} c_2^{\beta})^{\mu}, \qquad 0 < \beta, \quad \mu < 1$$

It can be verified that the function representing the demand for the second commodity, derived from (10.9), is given by

(10.9a)
$$c_2(\alpha) = \beta \frac{I(\alpha)}{\bar{p}(\alpha)}$$

where $I(\alpha)$ is the disposable income in state α.

Differentiating (10.9a) and multiplying by $tp(\alpha)$, we obtain

(10.9b)
$$tp(\alpha)c_{21}(\alpha) = \beta \frac{t}{1+t}$$

Substituting (10.9b) into (10.7) yields $\tilde{q} = \overline{q}$. This means that when commodity preferences are represented by a Cobb–Douglas utility function, the optimal policy calls for no intervention in the purchase of real equities.

Although we do not know which type of real-equity purchases should be taxed in order to support the optimal allocation, we can show that if equity purchases of the import-competing industry have to be taxed, the tax rate should be smaller than the tariff rate. This is equivalent to saying that the investors' relative real-equity price $\tilde{q}$ should be larger than the producers' relative price q.

In order to prove the last statement, divide (10.7) by $(1 + t)$ to obtain

$$q = \frac{Ev_1(\alpha)\overline{p}(\alpha)\theta_2(\alpha)[1 + t - t\overline{p}(\alpha)c_{21}(\alpha)]^{-1}}{Ev_1(\alpha)\theta_1(\alpha)[1 - tp(\alpha)c_{21}(\alpha)]^{-1}}$$

$$= \frac{Ev_1(\alpha)\overline{p}(\alpha)\theta_2(\alpha)[1 + t\{1 - m_2(\alpha)\}]^{-1}}{Ev_1(\alpha)\theta_1(\alpha)[1 - tp(\alpha)c_{21}(\alpha)]^{-1}}$$

$$= \frac{Ev_1(\alpha)\overline{p}(\alpha)\theta_2(\alpha)[1 + tm_1(\alpha)]^{-1}}{Ev_1(\alpha)\theta_1(\alpha)[1 - tp(\alpha)c_{21}(\alpha)]^{-1}}$$

$$< \frac{Ev_1(\alpha)\overline{p}(\alpha)\theta_2(\alpha)}{Ev_1(\alpha)\theta_1(\alpha)}$$

$$= \tilde{q}$$

where $m_i(\alpha)$ is the marginal propensity to consume commodity i in state α, which is positive due to our normality assumption. The last equality is obtained from (10.8).

The analysis of this section can also be applied to the case of no international trade in securities. In that case, it can also be shown that the investors' $\tilde{q}$ should exceed the producers' relative real-equity price. Since there is no trade in securities, the wedge between the investors' and producers' prices can be secured by a tax on the purchase of type-2 real equities. In this case, however, we cannot determine the impact of the tax on resource flows between the two industries.

Let us conclude this section by examining our results in the limiting case of full certainty. In this case, (10.7) and (10.8) imply $\tilde{q} = \overline{q}$; we also have $\bar{q} = \bar{p}$ and $q = p$, with assets–indifference curves which are straight lines with slope $\bar{p}$. The stock market equilibrium of an economy is described in Figure 10.4.

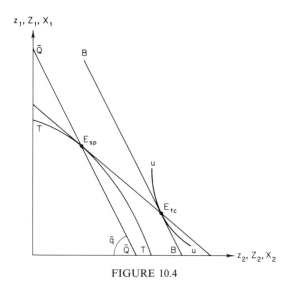

FIGURE 10.4

Production takes place at E_{sp} where the marginal rate of transformation equals q. $\bar{Q}\bar{Q}$ is the assets–budget line whose slope is $\bar{q}$ $[=(1 + t)q = (1 + t)p]$. The assets–indifference curves are represented by lines which are parallel to $\bar{Q}\bar{Q}$. Hence, any point along $\bar{Q}\bar{Q}$ is an optimal portfolio point, so line $\bar{Q}\bar{Q}$ also describes portfolio income. However, consumers receive lump-sum transfers which equal tariff proceeds. Disposable income is represented by BB, where BB is parallel to $\bar{Q}\bar{Q}$, and the consumer chooses E_{tc} as his optimal consumption bundle.

Now, commodities are exchanged with the rest of the world at p units of good 1 per unit of good 2. The line $E_{sp}E_{tc}$, whose slope is p $(= q)$, represents these trading opportunities. Hence, the situation described in Figure 10.4 is an equilibrium situation. It is also clear from Figure 10.4 that the allocation (E_{sp}, E_{tc}) is optimal, provided no intervention is permitted in commodity markets.

In more traditional terms, Figure 10.4 describes a situation in which producers of commodity 2 pay a commodity tax whose rate just equals the tariff rate. This is, of course, the optimal policy if only producers can be taxed. In the certainty case, the stock market obviously plays no significant role, but we have chosen to present this discussion in order to show the connection between our analysis and the traditional one.

10.3 OPTIMAL INTERVENTION IN THE PRESENCE OF CONFISCATION RISKS

In this section we consider a rather unorthodox problem which is intimately related to international trade in securities. It can be argued that investments abroad are not equivalent to domestic investments, because foreign investments bear the additional risk that their returns may be confiscated. Will market forces fully take into account this possibility, or is there room for a welfare-improving intervention in capital markets?

Keynes expressed the following view on this issue[2]:

> Consider two investments, the one at home and the other abroad, with equal risks of repudiation or confiscation or legislation restricting profit. It is a matter of indifference to the individual investor which he selects. But the nation as a whole retains in the one case the object of the investment and the fruits of it; whilst in the other case both are lost. If a loan to improve a South American Capital is repudiated, we, as a nation, still have the houses. If the Grand Trunk Railway of Canada fails its shareholders by reason of legal restriction of the rates chargeable, or for any other cause, we have nothing. If the Underground System of London fails its shareholders, Londoners still have their Underground System.

Keynes identifies here a divergence between private and social benefits in foreign investments, which can be corrected by public intervention. We show that in a related problem in which there is a positive probability of confiscation of returns on foreign security holdings, a subsidy should be given to exported securities. This is required in order to correct external effects which exist in such situations and which put a wedge between marginal private and social valuations. The precise nature of these externalities will now be explained.

---

[2] See Kemp (1964, p. 200). It does not seem to be important whether we deal with foreign security holdings or direct investment abroad.

Consider a situation in which the international flow of profits is discontinued with probability π. This can result from a foreign confiscation of the returns on foreign security holdings of the home country. We shall assume that in such cases the home country retaliates by not paying out dividends to foreigners and that these dividends are paid out to local stockholders as lump-sum transfers.[3]

We assume that the probability of the suspension of dividend flows is independent of the state of the world which realizes, as well as of the volume of security trade. Usually, one may expect π to depend on the volume of equities exchanged between the home country and foreigners. If foreigners are averse to control by the home country over their industries, the probability of their suspending dividend flows may increase with the share of ownership of foreign industries by the home country. On the other hand, the larger the exchange of equities, the more foreigners will lose as a result of such a disruption. Hence, it is not clear how π changes with the volume of equity trade, so we assume that it is constant.[4]

The assumption that π does not depend on the state of the world is more disturbing. One can expect confiscation in the states of the world in which the net flow of dividends is favorable to the home country (remember that in some states of the world the home country gets a net inflow of dividends, while in other states it experiences a net outflow). But by the same argument, the home country may also wish to discontinue dividend payments in some states of the world.

Now, if every country confiscates dividend payments in states of the world which are unfavorable to it, security trade will be eliminated. We assume here that foreigners initiate a confiscation after the exchange of securities takes place and before the realization of a state of the world. If the confiscation decision is known before trade in securities takes place, it eliminates the incentive to trade in securities—a case which is not interesting. Hence, the confiscation decision is assumed to take place only after the exchange of securities. On the other hand, the fact that the confiscation takes place before the realization of α makes the

[3] If foreign-owned dividends are confiscated and paid out to local stockholders according to their relative shares in domestic industries, the problem is not significantly different, but the optimal policy is modified.

[4] The same argument applies to Bhagwati and Srinivasan (1976) who consider a disruption of trade in commodities. If the probability of trade disruption is assumed to depend on the volume of equity exchange with the rest of the world, there is an argument for intervention which is similar to the one discussed in the first section of this chapter (concerning the monopoly power of a country in trade).

disruption–nondisruption distribution independent of the distribution of α.

Since the home country is small, we assume a given distribution of commodity prices, and that this distribution is independent of whether dividends are confiscated.

Naturally, the confiscation problem is more relevant for a large country than for a small one. However, our purpose is to isolate factors which may require intervention in capital markets and which do not stem from monopoly power. If a country has monopoly power in trade in securities, there is a clear case for an optimal tax on security imports which is similar to an optimal tariff, as shown in the first section of this chapter.

We now present the formal model. If π, the probability of confiscation, is equal to zero, then an owner of one equity of type j pays q_j and receives the vector of returns $[p_j(1)\theta_j(1), \ldots, p_j(S)\theta_j(S)]$. This is independent of whether the equity owner is a domestic or foreign resident, and of whether he is a holder of a domestic or foreign equity.

If π is positive, we have to distinguish between foreign and domestic residents, as well as between foreign and domestic equities. A domestic resident holding a foreign real equity of type j receives the vector $[0, \ldots, 0]$ with probability π and the vector $[p_j(1)\theta_j(1), \ldots, p_j(S)\theta_j(S)]$ with probability $1 - \pi$. (This can also be looked upon as if the number of states is doubled, but we shall not adopt this approach.) A domestic resident holding a domestic real equity of type j receives the vector $[p_j(1)\theta_j(1), \ldots, p_j(S)\theta_j(S)]$ with probability one.

A foreign resident holding a domestic real equity of type j receives the vector $[0, \ldots, 0]$ with probability π, and the vector $[p_j(1)\theta_j(1), \ldots, p_j(S)\theta_j(S)]$ with probability $1 - \pi$.

Let q_j^F be the price of a foreign type-j real equity. This is the price which a foreign resident (as well as a domestic resident) has to pay for this security.

Let q_j^L be the price that foreigners are willing to pay for a domestic real equity of type j. The prices satisfy $q_j^F > q_j^L$, because a foreign owner of a foreign type-j real equity gets more than a foreign owner of a local type-j real equity in case of confiscation, and gets the same in case no confiscation takes place.

Finally, in case confiscation takes place, local residents receive lump-sum transfers which are equal to the locally confiscated dividends.

If there is no intervention in financial capital markets, producers choose a production pattern $[\hat{Z}_1(Z_2^0), Z_2^0]$ at which the marginal rate of transformation equals q_2/q_1^F, assuming that type-2 real equities are imported.[5] q_2 is the price of domestic type-2 real equities. (We shall relate it to $q_2{}^L$ and $q_2{}^F$ after presenting the consumer problem.) On the other hand, domestic investors solve in equilibrium the problem

(10.10)   choose $z_1{}^L, z_2{}^L, z_1{}^F, z_2{}^F \geq 0$

to maximize

$$\pi Ev[p(\alpha); \theta_1(\alpha)z_1{}^L + p(\alpha)\theta_2(\alpha)z_2{}^L + T(\alpha)]$$
$$+ (1 - \pi)Ev[p(\alpha); \theta_1(\alpha)(z_1{}^L + z_1{}^F) + p(\alpha)\theta_2(\alpha)(z_2{}^L + z_2{}^F)]$$

subject to

$$q_1{}^L z_1{}^L + q_2 z_2{}^L + q_1{}^F z_1{}^F + q_2{}^F z_2{}^F \leq q_1{}^L \hat{Z}_1(Z_2{}^0) + q_2 Z_2{}^0$$

$T(\alpha)$ consists of confiscated foreign dividends in case confiscation takes place, $z_j{}^L$ is domestic holdings of domestic type-j real equities, and $z_j{}^F$ is domestic holdings of foreign type-j real equities, $j = 1,2$.

Observe that for the proposed prices and pattern of trade to reflect an equilibrium situation, $z_2{}^L = Z_2{}^0$ has to solve (10.10), and $z_2{}^F$ which solves (10.10) has to be positive. Hence, since a unit of $z_2{}^L$ provides a higher marginal expected utility than a unit of $z_2{}^F$, the fact that the investor chooses positive quantities of both of them implies $q_2 > q_2{}^F$ ($> q_2{}^L$).

Now, since $q_1{}^F > q_1{}^L$ and a unit of $z_1{}^L$ provides a higher marginal expected utility than a unit of $z_1{}^F$, the investor will choose to abstain from foreign purchases of type-1 real equities; that is, $z_1{}^F = 0$ solves (10.10).

The investors take $T(\alpha)$ as given (as a lump-sum transfer). But $T(\alpha)$ depends on the pattern of production and aggregate portfolio composition. In particular,

(10.11) $$T(\alpha) \equiv \theta_1(\alpha)[\hat{Z}_1(Z_2) - z_1{}^L]$$

where we substitute $Z_2{}^0$ for Z_2 in (10.10). The right-hand side of (10.11) describes the dividends that have to be paid out to foreign investors in state α in the absence of confiscation (remember that foreigners invest only in the first industry).

It can be seen now that the competitive equilibrium is inefficient. When a domestic investor considers a marginal increase in $z_1{}^L$, he does not take into account its effect on $T(\alpha)$. However, if the community increases $z_1{}^L$, confiscated foreign dividends will decline. Hence, the

---

[5] We have chosen a particular pattern of trade in securities in order to simplify the exposition. It is also possible to use the opposite pattern of trade.

price $q_1{}^L$ underestimates the marginal cost of an increase in $z_1{}^L$; that is, the social marginal cost of holding $z_1{}^L$ exceeds the private marginal cost of holding $z_1{}^L$. This means that optimality requires that the investor pay more than $q_1{}^L$ for domestic type-1 real equities. It is also efficient in this case to have the producers' price equal the investors' price, since there are no external effects between producers and investors. Hence, the optimal policy calls for a subsidy to exports of equities (type-1 real equities if we assume that the optimal policy does not reverse the pattern of security trade). The optimal subsidy equals the social value of the decline in $T(\alpha)$ which results from a marginal increase in $z_1{}^L$. Hence, the optimal subsidy per equity is

$$(10.12) \quad \mathrm{sub}_1 = \frac{1}{\mu}\, \pi E v_1 [\, p(\alpha);\ \theta_1(\alpha) z_1{}^L + p(\alpha)\theta_2(\alpha) z_2{}^L + T(\alpha)]\theta_1(\alpha)$$

where μ is the marginal expected utility of wealth, and everything is evaluated at the optimal allocation. For a detailed derivation of this result, see Appendix B.

It is difficult to assess the impact of the optimal policy on resource allocation. The transition from an equilibrium without intervention to an equilibrium with optimal intervention involves both real-income and substitution effects. These effects may work in opposite directions as far as resource allocation is concerned.

Consider, for example, domestic holdings of domestic type-2 real equities. (The following discussion relies on compensated demand functions.) The increase in real income (expected utility) associated with the transition from a suboptimal to an optimal allocation may increase or decrease the demand for this security, because in portfolio problems the income effect is not unambiguously signed [see, for example, Cass and Stiglitz (1972)]. In addition, we have two price effects. The increase in the price of $z_1{}^L$ generates a substitution effect whose nature is unknown; it is not clear whether the optimal price of $z_2{}^L$ is larger or smaller than q_2, so even the own-price effect cannot be evaluated. Since local holdings of local type-2 real equities are just equal to Z_2, this means that the flow of resources in the production sectors is also ambiguous.

The difficulties just described can perhaps be best demonstrated by means of Figure 10.5. EF represents the transformation curve between Z_1 and Z_2. The slopes of FG and HI are $q_2{}^F/q_1{}^L$, describing the rate of exchange of $z_2{}^F$ for $z_1{}^L$ through foreign trade. This is determined by

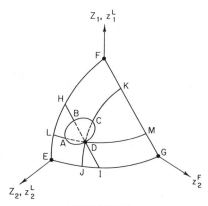

FIGURE 10.5

the rest of the world. The ruled surface EFG represents the boundary of the feasible portfolio set of the economy.

Suppose that D is the equilibrium point without intervention, and that the circular line $ABCD$ describes the intersection of EFG with the indifference surface which passes through D.[6] The indifference surface has to cut into EFG in the direction of the z_1^L axis, because the marginal social valuation of z_1^L is smaller than the private one. The private valuation in terms of z_2^L is represented by the slope of JK at D ($=$ the slope of EF at H) and, in terms of z_2^F, by the slope of HI ($=$ the slope of FG) at D. It can also be shown that the slope $-dz_2^F/dz_2^L$ of the indifference surface at point D is smaller than the slope of LM at D. Hence, $ABCD$ has to have a portion below LM. (It need not, however, have the portion to the right of JK.)

Now, the optimal point is somewhere within the circular line $ABCD$. If it happens to be to the right of JK, then the transition from D to the optimal point involves a decline in the output of the second

---

[6] This indifference surface consists of all the combinations of (z_1^L, z_2^L, z_2^F) for which

$$\pi Ev[p(\alpha); \theta_1(\alpha)\hat{Z}_1(z_2^L) + p(\alpha)\theta_2(\alpha)z_2^L] \qquad + (1 - \pi)Ev[p(\alpha); \theta_1(\alpha)z_1^L$$
$$+ p(\alpha)\theta_2(\alpha)(z_2^L + z_2^F)] = \text{constant}$$

at the equilibrium expected utility level. Observe that it is convex to the origin. The surface EFG is implicitly defined by

$$q_2^F z_2^F + q_1^L z_1^L - q_1^L \hat{Z}_1(z_2^L) = 0$$
$$(z_1^L, z_2^L, z_2^F) \geq 0$$

industry and in local type-2 real-equity holdings. However, local holdings of foreign type-2 real equities increase, and so do local and foreign holdings of local type-1 real equities. If the optimal point happens to be within *BCD*, local holdings of foreign equities and foreign holdings of local equities both decline, while resources move from the second to the first industry. It is also easy to see what happens when the optimal point is either in *ABD* or below *LM*, so we shall not describe it. Note, however, that when the optimal point lies to the left of *BD*, the export subsidy to type-1 real equities leads to a *decline* in the output of industry 1, while when the optimal point lies below *CD*, the optimal policy increases the exchange of securities with the rest of the world.

REFERENCES

Baldwin, R. E. (1948). Equilibrium in international trade: A diagrammatic analysis, *Quarterly Journal of Economics* **62**, 748–762.

Baldwin, R. E. (1952). The new welfare economics and gains in international trade, *Quarterly Journal of Economics* **66**, 91–101.

Bhagwati, J., and Srinivasan, T. N. (1976). Optimal trade policy and compensation under endogenous uncertainty: The phenomenon of market disruption, *Journal of International Economics* **6**, 317–336.

Cass, D., and Stiglitz, T. E. (1972). Risk aversion and wealth effects on portfolios with many assets, *Review of Economic Studies* **39**, 331–354.

Jones, R. W. (1967). International capital movements and the theory of tariffs and trade, *Quarterly Journal of Economics* **81**, 1–38.

Kemp, M. C. (1964). "The Pure Theory of International Trade." Prentice-Hall, Englewood Cliffs, New Jersey.

Kemp, M. C. (1966). The gain from international trade and investment: A neo-Heckscher–Ohlin approach, *American Economic Review* **56**, 788–809.

Chapter 11

A Dynamic Reformulation

So far our analysis was confined to a two-period world; after the second period the world ceases to exist or just repeats itself. In this framework there is no trade-off between consumption and portfolio investment. Although the choice of portfolio is dictated by preferences over consumption, it is not possible to increase consumption at the expense of security purchase. This means that savings, as defined in the usual sense, are absent. Hence, this model has some static features.

In this chapter we suggest a dynamic extension in order to remedy these shortcomings. Our extended version contains an infinite horizon and introduces explicitly the trade-off between present period consumption and savings. We shall show that the dynamic version preserves some important characteristics of the two-period model. We shall also present an example which illustrates an equilibrium structure of the dynamic model.

11.1 THE MODEL

Let the intertemporal von Neumann–Morgenstern utility function of the home country be

$$(11.1) \qquad U = \sum_{t=0}^{\infty} (\delta)^t u(c_1{}^t, c_2{}^t), \qquad 0 < \delta < 1$$

where δ is a discount factor (which is equal to one over one plus the rate of time preference) and superscript t denotes a variable in time t. For example, c_1^t is consumption of the first good in period t. This convention is also used below.

We denote now by α^t a state in period t. A state of the world is described by the infinite sequence $(\alpha^1, \alpha^2, \ldots, \alpha^t, \ldots)$. We assume that the set of states and the distribution over it are the same in each period. Put differently, α^t can be considered as an identical independently distributed random variable for all t.

We assume also that equities are one-period securities. This means that the purchase of an equity today entitles its holder only to the equity's share in profits tomorrow. After the distribution of profits, the equity has no more economic value. In every period, firms issue one-period equities in order to finance factor payments.

Given the portfolio composition from period $t - 1$, (z_1^{t-1}, z_2^{t-1}), portfolio income in state α^t in period t is

$$(11.2) \qquad z^t(\alpha^t) = p_1^t(\alpha^t)\theta_1(\alpha^t)z_1^{t-1} + p_2^t(\alpha^t)\theta_2(\alpha^t)z_2^{t-1}$$

The income of factors of production in period t, in state α^t, is equal to the value of newly issued equities by the home firms:

$$(11.3) \qquad Z^t(\alpha^t) = q_1^t(\alpha^t)\{Z_1[q^t(\alpha^t)] + q^t(\alpha^t)Z_2[q^t(\alpha^t)]\}$$

(We omit factor endowments (L, K) in writing the supply functions $Z_i[\cdot]$.)

The home country can choose in period t–state α^t consumption and new equity purchase whose total value does not exceed portfolio plus factor incomes. Hence, the period t–state α^t budget constraint is

$$
\begin{aligned}
(11.4) \quad & p_1^t(\alpha^t)c_1^t(\alpha^t) + p_2^t(\alpha^t)c_2^t(\alpha^t) + q_1^t(\alpha^t)[z_1^t(\alpha^t) + q^t(\alpha^t)z_2(\alpha^t)] \\
& \leq p_1^t(\alpha^t)\theta_1(\alpha^t)z_1^{t-1} + p_2^t(\alpha^t)\theta_2(\alpha^t)z_2^{t-1} \\
& \quad + q_1^t(\alpha^t)\{Z_1[q^t(\alpha^t)] + q^t(\alpha^t)Z_2[q^t(\alpha^t)]\} \\
& = z^t(\alpha^t) + Z^t(\alpha^t)
\end{aligned}
$$

In our two-period model, we had two numeraires; a numeraire for the first period and a numeraire for the second period. The only relative prices that mattered were relative commodity prices and relative security prices. There was no significance to a price of a good in terms of a security, or vice versa. This was of course a result of the structure in which securities were traded in one period and goods were traded in another period; goods and securities were never traded simultaneously.

Now the situation is different, as one can see from (11.4). Goods and securities are traded simultaneously in every period. Observe, however, that in the case of certainty it is still true that the relative price of goods is equal to the relative price of securities; the relative price of securities today has to be equal to the relative price of goods tomorrow (from arbitrage considerations). Suppose also that in the case of certainty the relative price of goods is the same in every period. Then the relative price of equities today equals the relative price of goods today. Does this imply that commodity prices equal equity prices? The answer is no, since the difference between the increase over time in the absolute price levels of goods and securities reflects the interest rate, which is positive due to time preference.

The problem of the economy now is to maximize the expected value of (11.1) subject to the infinite sequence of budget constraints (11.4). This is a dynamic programming problem which can be solved by means of Bellman's principle of optimality.

Let $V^t(z_1^{t-1}, z_2^{t-1}, \alpha^t)$ be the maximum of

$$E \sum_{\tau=t}^{\infty} (\delta)^{\tau-t} u[c_1(\alpha^\tau), c_2(\alpha^\tau)]$$

subject to (11.4) with τ substituted for t. Then, we have by the principle of optimality (omitting α^t from $c_1^t, c_2^t, z_1^t, z_2^t$)

(11.5) $\quad V^t(z_1^{t-1}, z_2^{t-1}, \alpha^t)$
$$= \max[u(c_1, c_2) + \delta \underset{\alpha^{t+1}}{E} V^{t+1}(z_1^t, z_2^t, \alpha^{t+1})], \quad t = 0, 1, \ldots$$

subject to the single-period budget constraint (11.4) and $(c_1^t, c_2^t, z_1^t, z_2^t) \geq 0$. An α^{t+1} below E indicates that the expectation is over α^{t+1}.

This implies that, given the functions $V^t(\cdot), t = 1, 2, \ldots$, the economy chooses consumption, savings, and its portfolio composition so as to solve in period t and state α^t the single-period problem

(11.6) $\quad$ choose $\quad c_1^t(\alpha^t), c_2^t(\alpha^t), z_1^t(\alpha^t), z_2^t(\alpha^t) \geq 0$

to maximize

$U^t[c_1^t(\alpha^t), c_2^t(\alpha^t), z_1^t(\alpha^t), z_2^t(\alpha^t)]$
$$\equiv u[c_1^t(\alpha^t), c_2^t(\alpha^t)] + \delta \underset{\alpha^{t+1}}{E} V^{t+1}[z_1^t(\alpha^t), z_2^t(\alpha^t), \alpha^{t+1}]$$

subject to (11.4)

$U^t(\cdot)$ represents the preferences of period t over consumption and equities. We now present a diagrammatic exposition of the solution to (11.6). However, before we do so it may prove useful to consider the accounts of the balance of payments in this setup.

Let $X^t(\alpha^t)$ be the value of commodity sales in period t and state α^t of the home country. $X^t(\alpha^t)$ depends on the allocation of factors of production in period $t - 1$ and the realization of commodity prices and the technological parameters in period t:

$$X^t(\alpha^t) = p_1{}^t(\alpha^t)\theta_1(\alpha^t)Z_1^{t-1} + p_2{}^t(\alpha^t)\theta_2(\alpha^t)Z_2^{t-1}$$

$X^t(\alpha^t)$ is also equal to the dividend payments of the industries of the home country in period t and state α^t.

Let

$$C^t(\alpha^t) = p_1{}^t(\alpha^t)c_1{}^t(\alpha^t) + p_2{}^t(\alpha^t)c_2{}^t(\alpha^t)$$

be the value of consumption and

$$K^t(\alpha^t) = q_1{}^t(\alpha^t)z_1{}^t(\alpha^t) + q_2{}^t(\alpha^t)z_2{}^t(\alpha^t)$$

the value of security purchase in period t and state α^t. Then, using the definitions of $z^t(\alpha^t)$ and $Z^t(\alpha^t)$, dividend income and factor income [see (11.2) and (11.3)], (11.4) can be rewritten as

(11.7) $C^t(\alpha^t) - z^t(\alpha^t) + K^t(\alpha^t) - Z^t(\alpha^t) = 0$

Adding and subtracting $X^t(\alpha^t)$ from the left-hand side of (11.7), we get

(11.8) $[C^t(\alpha^t) - X^t(\alpha^t)] + [X^t(\alpha^t) - z^t(\alpha^t)]$
$$+ [K^t(\alpha^t) - Z^t(\alpha^t)] = 0$$

Equation (11.8) represents the balance of payments accounts. The term in the first set of brackets represents the trade account deficit, the term in the second set represents the service account deficit (net dividend outflows), and the last term represents the capital account deficit (net equity purchase). The sum of the deficits in the trade and service accounts is $C^t(\alpha^t) - z^t(\alpha^t)$ and it is equal to the deficit in the current account. If there is no international trade in securities, then in equilibrium, $Z_i{}^t = z_i{}^t$, $i = 1, 2$, and the deficits in the capital and service accounts are zero.

11.2   A DIAGRAMMATIC EXPOSITION

For the purpose of the diagrammatic exposition, let us aggregate consumption into the Hicks composite good $C^t(\alpha^t)$. Then, we can

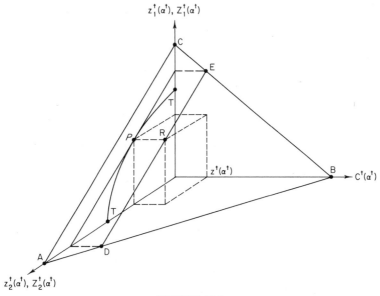

FIGURE 11.1

represent the budget constraint of the economy (11.4) by the plane ABC in Figure 11.1. The construction of this plane is as follows. Its slopes have to reflect relative prices. Hence, because of our aggregation of consumption, the slope of CB toward the $C^t(\alpha^t)$ axis is $1/q_1{}^t(\alpha^t)$, and the slope of AB toward the same axis is $1/[q_1{}^t(\alpha^t)q^t(\alpha^t)] = 1/q_2{}^t(\alpha^t)$. The slope of AC toward the $z_2{}^t(\alpha^t)$ axis is $q^t(\alpha^t)$. It remains, therefore, to determine only the height of the plane. This can be done by choosing a feasible point at which (11.4) is satisfied with equality.

We have drawn in Figure 11.1 the transformation curve between $Z_1{}^t$ and $Z_2{}^t$. Given $q^t(\alpha^t)$, production is chosen at point P, at which a line parallel to AC is tangent to the transformation curve. Clearly, since $z^t(\alpha^t) > 0$, the economy can choose a portfolio which consists of $(Z_1{}^t, Z_2{}^t)$ and consume the income from dividends; that is, choose $C^t(\alpha^t) = z^t(\alpha^t)$. This choice is represented by point R, where R lies on a horizontal line through P and the distance between R and P equals $z^t(\alpha^t)$.

We can now impose the preference map generated by $U^t(\cdot)$ on Figure 11.1 in order to find the optimal portfolio and consumption point $[U^t(\cdot)$ has to be modified in the usual way in order to represent aggregate consumption$]$.

If there is no international trade in equities, then equilibrium security prices are such that the optimal point is R. In this case investors hold the domestically issued equities and the value of consumption equals portfolio income, just as in the two-period model. The deficits in each of the three balance of payments accounts are zero.

If there is international trade in securities, then any point on ABC can be an equilibrium point. If the equilibrium point is to the right of DE, that is, $C^t(\alpha^t) > z^t(\alpha^t)$, then there is a deficit in the current account and a surplus in the capital account. If the equilibrium point lies to the left of DE, then there is a surplus in the current account and a deficit in the capital account.

11.3   THE BASIC PROPOSITIONS

It is clear from the discussion in the previous section that our conclusions from Chapter 7, concerning the basic propositions of international trade theory, are valid in the present framework. If there is no international trade in securities, countries need not specialize according to comparative advantage in the Ricardian model, and in the Heckscher–Ohlin model factor prices need not be equalized, and the Stolper–Samuelson and Rybczynski theorems need not hold. If, however, there is international trade in equities, these propositions are restored. One has to be careful only to formulate the Stolper–Samuelson and Rybczynski theorems in terms of equity prices instead of commodity prices. Observe that an important feature of the two-period model is preserved here; that is, the allocation of production resources depends on relative equity prices (which in turn determine factor prices) and not on commodity prices. This happens despite the fact that consumption does take place simultaneously with production.

An additional remark on the Stolper–Samuelson theorem is in order. In the two-period model with trade in equities, an increase in the price of an equity, other things being equal, increases the real reward of one factor and reduces the real reward of the other factor, where real rewards are measured in terms of equities. However, given a constant distribution of commodity prices, the gaining factor can increase proportionately its equity holdings and thus assure itself of more consumption in the second period in every state of the world. In the present context, the gaining factor can buy in the present period both more equities and more consumption.

11.4 AN EXAMPLE

We present now an example of a two-country world for which we are able to work out a stationary equilibrium. In this equilibrium the commodity prices have a genuine distribution which is the same in every period, while equity prices are constant over time and across states. The allocation of factors of production and the composition of portfolios are also constant over time and across states, but consumption and commodity trade levels are random variables with an identical independent distribution in every period.

Let the temporal utility functions of the home and foreign countries be

$$(11.9) \qquad u(c_1, c_2) = -(1 - \beta) \log(1 - \beta) - \beta \log \beta$$
$$+ (1 - \beta) \log c_1 + \beta \log c_2, \qquad 0 < \beta < 1$$

$$(11.10) \quad u^*(c_1{}^*, c_2{}^*) = -(1 - \beta^*) \log(1 - \beta^*) - \beta^* \log \beta^*$$
$$+ (1 - \beta^*) \log c_1{}^* + \beta^* \log c_2{}^*, \qquad 0 < \beta^* < 1$$

and let $\theta_i(\alpha)$, $i = 1, 2$, be (genuine) independent identically distributed random variables which are the same for both countries. Every country has its own transformation curve between real equities. These transformation curves are summarized by the supply functions $Z_i(q)$, $Z_i{}^*(q^*)$, $i = 1, 2$ (see Chapter 5).

Let us begin with the case in which there is no international trade in securities. In this case $z_i = Z_i(q)$, $z_i{}^* = Z_i{}^*(q^*)$, $i = 1, 2$, is satisfied in every equilibrium. This implies that the value of consumption of each country is equal to its portfolio income. But, under these circumstances, commodity market clearing conditions imply the same structure of returns on both types of equities, as we have shown in Chapter 7 [see (7.20) and (7.21)]. In particular, it is shown there that in this case

$$(11.11) \qquad \frac{\theta_2(\alpha)p_2(\alpha)}{\theta_1(\alpha)p_1(\alpha)} = \frac{\beta z_1 + \beta^* z_1{}^*}{Z_2 + Z_2{}^* - \beta z_2 - \beta^* z_2}$$
$$= q$$
$$= q^*$$

is a necessary condition for equilibrium [see (7.17) and (7.21)].

We want to show that there is a stationary equilibrium in which the portfolio composition of each country is constant; state and time independent. In this case, since there is no international trade in equities, (11.11) implies

(11.12) $q = q^*$

$$= \frac{\beta Z_1(q) + \beta^* Z_1{}^*(q)}{(1 - \beta)Z_2(q) + (1 - \beta^*)Z_2{}^*(q)}$$

Now, since $Z_1(q)$ and $Z_1{}^*(q)$ are declining in q and both reach zero for sufficiently high values of q, and since $Z_2(q)$ and $Z_2{}^*(q)$, are increasing in q and both reach zero at a sufficiently low value of q, there is a unique value $\bar{q}$ for which (11.12) is satisfied. It is therefore clear that if there is an equilibrium of the type for which we are looking, it has to satisfy

(11.13) $q = q^* = \bar{q}$

(11.14) $Z_i^t = \bar{Z}_i \equiv Z_i(\bar{q}),$ $i = 1, 2$

(11.15) $Z_i^{*^t} = \bar{Z}_i{}^* \equiv Z_i{}^*(\bar{q}),$ $i = 1, 2$

(11.16) $\theta_2(\alpha^t)p_2{}^t(\alpha^t) = p_1{}^t(\alpha^t)\theta_1(\alpha^t)\bar{q},$

$$\alpha^t = 1, 2, \ldots, S, \quad t = 0, 1, \ldots$$

We are free to choose a numeraire in every state–period combination. The normalization we choose is

(11.17) $p_1{}^t(\alpha^t) = \dfrac{1}{\theta_1(\alpha^t)},$ $\alpha^t = 1, 2, \ldots, S, \quad t = 0, 1, \ldots$

This together with (11.16) implies

(11.18) $p_2{}^t(\alpha^t) = \dfrac{\bar{q}}{\theta_2(\alpha^t)},$ $\alpha^t = 1, 2, \ldots, S, \quad t = 0, 1, \ldots$

Hence, the distribution of our prices is stationary; it is the same in every period.

It remains to determine the absolute prices of equities. Let

(11.19) $q_1 = \delta$ $\Rightarrow$ $q_2 = \delta\bar{q}$

(11.20) $q_1{}^* = \delta^*$ $\Rightarrow$ $q_2{}^* = \delta^*\bar{q}$

It remains to show that there exist $V^t(\cdot), t = 0, 1, \ldots$, such that $z_i^t(\alpha^t) = \bar{Z}_i, i = 1, 2$, and

(11.21) $c_1^t(\alpha^t) = \dfrac{(1 - \beta)[p_1^t(\alpha^t)\theta_1(\alpha^t)\bar{Z}_1 + p_2^t(\alpha^t)\theta_2(\alpha^t)\bar{Z}_2]}{p_1^t(\alpha^t)}$

$\qquad\qquad = (1 - \beta)(\bar{Z}_1 + \bar{q}\bar{Z}_2)\theta_1(\alpha^t),$

$\qquad\qquad \alpha^t = 1, 2, \ldots, S, \quad t = 0, 1, \ldots$

(11.22) $c_2^t(\alpha^t) = \dfrac{\beta(\bar{Z}_1 + \bar{q}\bar{Z}_2)\theta_2(\alpha^t)}{\bar{q}},$

$\qquad\qquad \alpha^t = 1, 2, \ldots, S, \quad t = 0, 1, \ldots$

solve (11.5) for the home country, and that there exist $V^{*t}(\cdot), t = 0, 1, \ldots$, such that $z_i^{*t}(\alpha^t) = \bar{Z}_i^*, i = 1, 2$, and

(11.23) $c_1^{*t}(\alpha^t) = (1 - \beta^*)(\bar{Z}_1^* + \bar{q}\bar{Z}_2^*)\theta_1(\alpha^t),$

$\qquad\qquad \alpha^t = 1, 2, \ldots, S, \quad t = 0, 1, \ldots$

(11.24) $c_2^{*t}(\alpha^t) = \dfrac{\beta^*(\bar{Z}_1^* + \bar{q}\bar{Z}_2^*)\theta_2(\alpha^t)}{\bar{q}},$

$\qquad\qquad \alpha^t = 1, 2, \ldots, S, \quad t = 0, 1, \ldots$

solve (11.5) for the foreign country. It is easy to see that the commodity market clearing conditions are satisfied and that consumption levels are identically distributed in every period.

We show the solution to (11.5) only for the home country. The proof for the foreign country is the same.

Let $V^t(\cdot)$ be

(11.25) $V^t(z_1^{t-1}, z_2^{t-1}, \alpha^t) \equiv V(z_1^{t-1}, z_2^{t-1}, \alpha^t)$

$\qquad\qquad \equiv \log[\theta_1(\alpha^t)]^{1 - \beta}[\theta_2(\alpha^t)]^\beta(\bar{q})^{-\beta}$

$\qquad\qquad + \dfrac{\delta}{1 - \delta}\, E \log[\theta_1(\alpha)]^{1 - \beta}[\theta_2(\alpha)]^\beta(\bar{q})^{-\beta}$

$\qquad\qquad + \dfrac{1}{1 - \delta}\, \log[\delta(\bar{Z}_1 + \bar{q}\bar{Z}_2)$

$\qquad\qquad + (1 - \delta)(z_1^{t-1} + \bar{q}z_2^{t-1})],$

$\qquad\qquad \alpha^t = 1, 2, \ldots, S, \quad t = 0, 1, \ldots$

Then, it is easy to see that

$$(11.26) \quad \underset{\alpha^t}{EV}(z_1^{t-1}, z_2^{t-1}, \alpha^t) = \frac{1}{1-\delta} E \log[\theta_1(\alpha)]^{1-\beta}[\theta_2(\alpha)]^{\beta}(\bar{q})^{-\beta}$$

$$+ \frac{1}{1-\delta} \log \left[\delta(\bar{Z}_1 + \bar{q}\bar{Z}_2) \right.$$

$$+ (1-\delta)(z_1^{t-1} + \bar{q}z_2^{t-1})]$$

The reader can now verify that $E_{\alpha^0} V(\bar{Z}_1, \bar{Z}_2, \alpha^0)$ is the expected value of the discounted sum of utilities at our proposed allocation. The reader can also verify that, using (11.25), our proposed allocation solves (11.5) for our proposed prices. Hence, our prices and allocation constitute an equilibrium.

Our stationary solution can be represented in the framework of the two-period model. This is done in Figures 11.2 and 11.3. Each country has straight line assets–indifference curves with slope $\bar{q}$. These indifference curves are drawn in Figure 11.2a for the home country and in Figure 11.2b for the foreign country. Each country spends its income from dividends on consumption. Hence, it spends on securities its factor income. But given equity prices, producers choose the production point at the tangency of a line with slope $\bar{q}$ to the transformation curve. This line describes factor incomes and investors choose their portfolios on this line. Since assets–indifference curves are straight lines with slope $\bar{q}$, investors are indifferent between all points on the factor income line, and they may as well choose the points of tangency, E_s and E_s^*. This choice is repeated in every period independent of the state that realizes.

Figure 11.3 describes the state-α stationary consumption choice for the home country (the same applies to the foreign country).

Portfolio income in state α is given by the budget line BB whose slope is $p_2(\alpha)/p_1(\alpha) = \bar{q}\theta_1(\alpha)/\theta_2(\alpha)$. The consumer chooses his optimal consumption at the point of tangency of his temporal indifference curve and this budget line—point E_t. This choice depends only on the state that realizes; if the same state realizes in two different periods, then consumption and commodity trade will be the same in both periods.

It is now interesting to examine the structure of prices in our example. We have seen that relative equity prices are the same in both countries. It is therefore clear that factor prices in terms of equities

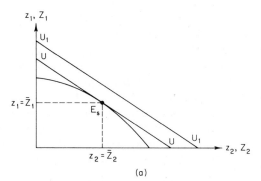

(a)

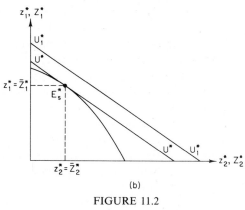

(b)

FIGURE 11.2

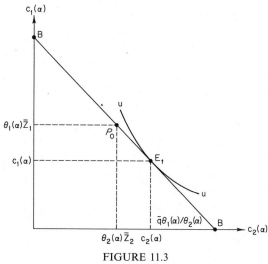

FIGURE 11.3

are also equal in both countries if they have the same production functions and no country specializes in production. Commodity prices are
certainly equal in both countries because of the trade in commodities.
But does this imply that factor prices in terms of commodities are
equalized? The answer is not necessarily so; that is, although relative
equity prices are the same, equity prices in terms of commodities need
not be the same. It is clear from (11.19) and (11.20) that equity prices are
equalized if and only if both countries have the same rates of time
preference; that is, $\delta = \delta^*$. If the rates of time preference are the same,
there will be both equity and factor price equalization, and if the rates of
time preference differ, there will be neither equity nor factor price
equalization [see Stiglitz (1970) for a discussion of factor price equalization in a deterministic dynamic model]. Observe, however, that in the
formulation of the example we have not required the production
functions to be the same in both countries; we only required the same
risk structure in the same sector of each country.

Consider the trade-off between present consumption and consumption in the next period. The consumer can buy a real equity of type 1
for δ dollars. This amounts to a sacrifice of the present consumption
of $\delta/p_1(\alpha^t) = \delta\theta_1(\alpha^t)$ units of good 1, given state α^t. The real equity
provides a sure return of one dollar in every state of the next period.
The purchasing power of the dollar in terms of good 1 depends,
however, on the state that will realize in the next period, and it is
equal to $1/p_1(\alpha^{t+1}) = \theta_1(\alpha^{t+1})$ in state α^{t+1}. This means that the consumer can replace the sure consumption of $\delta\theta_1(\alpha^t)$ units of good 1
today with the random consumption tomorrow of $\theta_1(\alpha^{t+1})$ units of
good 1. A similar calculation reveals that the sure consumption of
$\delta\theta_2(\alpha^t)$ units of commodity 2 today can be traded for a random consumption of $\theta_2(\alpha^{t+1})$ units of commodity 2 tomorrow.

Consider the case in which there is international trade in securities.
It is clear from the discussion in the last two paragraphs that if both
countries have the same rate of time preference, then the no security–
trade equilibrium is also an equilibrium in the presence of international
financial markets. However, if the rates of time preference differ, our
no security–trade equilibrium cannot be sustained in the presence of
international financial markets, because with trade in securities the
equity prices of the home country cannot differ from foreign equity
prices. What is then the nature of a stationary equilibrium when
countries have different rates of time preference? We shall show that
in this case there is an equilibrium price structure which is similar

but not identical to the price structure in the case of no trade in securities. But now the common price of type-1 real equities equals the largest discount factor; that is, if $\delta > \delta^*$, then $q_1 = \delta$, and the country with the lowest rate of time preference (largest discount factor) holds all financial assets. The other country holds no financial assets in this steady state and it consumes its factor income.

Assuming, without loss of generality, that the home country has a lower rate of time preference; that is, $\delta > \delta^*$, the equilibrium price structure is (the same prices prevail in both countries)

$$(11.27) \qquad q_1 = \delta > \delta^*$$

$$q_2 = \hat{q}\delta$$

$$(11.29) \qquad p_1{}^t(\alpha^t) = \frac{1}{\theta_1(\alpha^t)}, \qquad \alpha^t = 1, 2, \ldots, S, \quad t = 0, 1, \ldots$$

$$(11.30) \qquad p_2{}^t(\alpha^t) = \frac{\hat{q}}{\theta_2(\alpha^t)}, \qquad \alpha^t = 1, 2, \ldots, S, \quad t = 0, 1, \ldots$$

$$(11.31) \qquad \hat{Z}_i = Z_i(\hat{q}), \qquad\quad i = 1, 2$$

$$(11.32) \qquad \hat{Z}_i{}^* = Z_i{}^*(\hat{q}), \qquad\quad i = 1, 2$$

$$(11.33) \qquad \hat{z}_i = \hat{Z}_i + \hat{Z}_i{}^*, \qquad i = 1, 2$$

$$(11.34) \qquad \hat{z}_i{}^* = 0, \qquad\qquad i = 1, 2$$

$$(11.35) \qquad c_1{}^t(\alpha^t) = (1 - \beta)[\hat{Z}_1 + \hat{q}\hat{Z}_2 + (1 - \delta)(\hat{Z}_1{}^* + \hat{q}\hat{Z}_2{}^*)]\theta_1(\alpha^t),$$
$$\alpha^t = 1, 2, \ldots, S, \quad t = 0, 1, \ldots$$

$$(11.36) \qquad c_2{}^t(\alpha^t) = \frac{\beta[\hat{Z}_1 + \hat{q}\hat{Z}_2 + (1 - \delta)(\hat{Z}_1{}^* + \hat{q}\hat{Z}_2{}^*)]\theta_2(\alpha^t)}{\hat{q}},$$
$$\alpha^t = 1, 2, \ldots, S, \quad t = 0, 1, \ldots$$

$$(11.37) \qquad c_1^{*t}(\alpha^t) = (1 - \beta^*)\delta(\hat{Z}_1{}^* + \hat{q}\hat{Z}_2{}^*)\theta_1(\alpha^t),$$
$$\alpha^t = 1, 2, \ldots, S, \quad t = 0, 1, \ldots$$

$$(11.38) \qquad c_2^{*t}(\alpha^t) = \frac{\beta^*\delta(\hat{Z}_1{}^* + \hat{q}\hat{Z}_2{}^*)\theta_2(\alpha^t)}{\hat{q}},$$
$$\alpha^t = 1, 2, \ldots, S, \quad t = 0, 1, \ldots$$

Substituting the commodity demand functions into the commodity market clearing condition, we obtain, using (11.31)–(11.32),

$$(11.39) \qquad \hat{q} = \frac{\beta Z_1(\hat{q}) + [(1 - \delta)\beta + \delta\beta^*]Z_1^*(\hat{q})}{(1 - \beta)Z_2(\hat{q}) + [1 - (1 - \delta)\beta - \delta\beta^*]Z_2^*(\hat{q})}$$

There is a unique $\hat{q}$ for which (11.39) is satisfied (the proof is the same as that used to prove uniqueness of $\bar{q}$), and this is the equilibrium price of type-2 real equities in terms of type-1 real equities. Observe also that a comparison of (11.39) with (11.12) implies

$$(11.40) \qquad\qquad \hat{q} \gtreqqless \bar{q} \qquad \text{as} \quad \beta \gtreqqless \beta^*$$

Hence, if the home country has a stronger preference for the second commodity than the foreign country, the relative price of type-2 real equities will now be larger than in the case of no trade in securities and so will be the relative price of commodity 2, and if the foreign country has the stronger preference for the second commodity, q will now be lower and so will be $p_2(\alpha)/p_1(\alpha)$. If both countries have the same preference, then $\hat{q} = \bar{q}$ and there is no change in q as a result of the opening of international trade in equities. The reader can also see that in this case the price structure of the home country becomes the equilibrium price structure.

It remains to show that there exist functions $V^t(\cdot)$ and $V^{*t}(\cdot)$ for which the solution to (11.5), given the price structure, is (11.33)–(11.38). We present now the functions $V^{*t}(\cdot)$ (the functions $V^t(\cdot)$ are the same except that asterisks are omitted from the variables), and the reader can verify that the equilibrium allocation solves (11.5):

$$(11.41) \quad V^{*t}(z_1^{*t-1}, z_2^{*t-1}, \alpha^t) \equiv V^*(z_1^{*t-1}, z_2^{*t-1}, \alpha^t)$$

$$\equiv \log[\theta_1(\alpha^t)]^{1-\beta^*}[\theta_2(\alpha^t)]^{\beta^*}(\hat{q})^{-\beta^*}$$

$$+ \frac{\delta^*}{1-\delta^*} \underset{\alpha}{E} \log[\theta_1(\alpha)]^{1-\beta^*}[\theta_2(\alpha)]^{\beta^*}(\hat{q})^{-\beta^*}$$

$$+ \frac{1}{1-\delta^*} \log[\delta(\hat{Z}_1^* + \hat{q}\hat{Z}_2^*)$$

$$+ (1-\delta)(z_1^{*t-1} + \hat{q}z_2^{*t-1})]$$

$$\alpha^t = 1, 2, \ldots, S, \quad t = 0, 1, \ldots$$

Finally, let us comment on the likelihood of the existence of stationary solutions of the type presented in the example; that is, stationary solutions in which equity prices and factor allocations are state and time independent. We believe that this type of a stationary equilibrium will rarely exist, and that it may well be the case that the logarithmic utility function is the only one that yields it. The shape of the production functions is not important for this matter.

Our belief is based on the following reasoning. A necessary condition for (11.6) to have a solution with a state-independent portfolio choice is

(a) to have a utility function for which the marginal utility of income depends only on income, and
(b) to have state-independent income.

For income to be state independent, prices have to be proportional to the inverse of the technological coefficients, which seems to us can happen only with a Cobb–Douglas-type utility function. However, for a Cobb–Douglas-type utility function to have the marginal utility of income depend only on income, it has to be logarithmic.

REFERENCES

Stiglitz, J. E. (1970). Factor price equalization in a dynamic economy, *Journal of Political Economy* **78**, 456–488.

Appendix A

Derivation of Equation (8.15)

Consider the highest utility of the home country as a function of the tariff rate t:

(A.1) $\quad \hat{v}(\alpha, t) = v[(1 + t)p(\alpha); \theta_1(\alpha)z_1(t) + \theta_2(\alpha)p(\alpha)z_2{}^f(t)$
$$+ T(\alpha, t)]$$

where $T(\cdot)$, which represents tariff proceeds, is implicitly defined by

(A.2) $\quad T(\alpha, t) = tp(\alpha)\{c_2[(1 + t)p(\alpha); \theta_1(\alpha)z_1(t)$
$$+ \theta_2(\alpha)p(\alpha)z_2{}^f(t) + T(\alpha, t)] - \theta_2(\alpha)Z_2[(1 + t)q]\}$$

and where $z_1(t)$ is the domestic demand for type-1 real equities, and $z_2{}^f(t)$ the domestic demand for type-2 real equities measured in units of foreign type-2 real equities $[z_2{}^f(t) = (1 + t)z_2(t)]$.

From the assets–budget constraint

$$z_1(t) + qz_2{}^f(t) = Z[(1 + t)q]$$
$$\stackrel{\text{def}}{=} Z_1[(1 + t)q] + (1 + t)qZ_2[(1 + t)q]$$

which implies

(A.3) $\quad I(\alpha, t) \equiv \theta_1(\alpha)z_1(t) + \theta_2(\alpha)p(\alpha)z_2{}^f(t) + T(\alpha, t)$
$$= \theta_1(\alpha)Z[(1 + t)q] + [\theta_2(\alpha)p(\alpha) - \theta_1(\alpha)q]z_2{}^f(t) + T(\alpha, t)$$

Now, for small tariff rates, the welfare loss from the tariff can be approximated by the second-order Taylor expansion of $\hat{v}(\alpha, t)$ around $t = 0$, which is

(A.4) $E[\hat{v}(\alpha, t) - \hat{v}(\alpha, 0)] \cong tE\hat{v}_t(\alpha, 0) + \frac{1}{2}t^2 E\hat{v}_{tt}(\alpha, 0)$

In order to evaluate (A.4), we first differentiate (A.2) with respect to t, using (A.3), in order to calculate $T_t(\alpha, t)$:

(A.5) $T_t = \dfrac{p}{1 - tpc_{2I}} \{c_2 - \theta_2 Z_2 + t[pc_{2p}$

$$+ qc_{2I}\theta_1 Z_2 + c_{2I}(\theta_2 p - \theta_1 q)z_{2t}^f - q\theta_2 Z_2']\}$$

where c_{2p} is the derivative of c_2 with respect to its first argument, a prime indicates a derivative of the supply functions Z_i, and we use the identity

$$Z_1'[(1 + t)q] + (1 + t)qZ_2'[(1 + t)q] \equiv 0$$

From (A.5),

(A.6) $T_t(\alpha, 0) = p(\alpha)[c_2(\alpha, 0) - \theta_2(\alpha)Z_2(q)]$

Using (A.6) and the Slutzky decomposition $c_{2p} = c_{2p}^c - c_2 c_{2I}$, (A.5) yields

(A.7) $T_{tt}(\alpha, 0) = 2\{p(\alpha)^2 c_{2p}^c(\alpha, 0) - qp(\alpha)\theta_2(\alpha)Z_2'(q)$

$$+ p(\alpha)c_{2I}(\alpha, 0)[\theta_2(\alpha)p(\alpha)$$
$$- \theta_1(\alpha)q][z_{2t}^f(0) - Z_2(q)]\}$$

Equation (A.1) can also be written in the form

(A.8) $\hat{v}(\alpha, t) \equiv v[(1 + t)p(\alpha); I(\alpha, t)]$

Differentiating (A.8) twice, we get (using the property of the indirect utility function $\partial v/\partial[(1 + t)p] = -v_I c_2$ and the Slutzky decomposition)

(A.9) $\hat{v}_t(\alpha, t) = v_I(\alpha, t)[I_t(\alpha, t) - p(\alpha)c_2(\alpha, t)]$

(A.10) $\hat{v}_{tt}(\alpha, t) = v_I(\alpha, t)[I_{tt}(\alpha, t) - p(\alpha)^2 c_{2p}^c(\alpha, t)$

$$+ p(\alpha)^2 c_{2I}(\alpha, t)c_2(\alpha, t)$$
$$- p(\alpha)c_{2I}(\alpha, t)I_t(\alpha, t)] + [v_{Ip}(\alpha, t)p(\alpha)$$
$$+ v_{II}(\alpha, t)I_t(\alpha, t)][I_t(\alpha, t) - p(\alpha)c_2(\alpha, t)]$$

Now,

$$v_{\mathrm{Ip}} = v_{\mathrm{pI}} = \frac{\partial(-v_{\mathrm{I}}c_2)}{\partial I} = -v_{\mathrm{II}}c_2 - v_{\mathrm{I}}c_{2\mathrm{I}}$$

which, when substituted into (A.10), yields

(A.11) $\hat{v}_{tt}(\alpha, t) = v_{\mathrm{I}}(\alpha, t)[I_{tt}(\alpha, t) - p(\alpha)^2 c_{2\mathrm{p}}^c(\alpha, t)]$
  $- 2v_{\mathrm{I}}(\alpha, t)p(\alpha)c_{2\mathrm{I}}(\alpha, t)[I_t(\alpha, t) - p(\alpha)c_2(\alpha, t)]$
  $+ v_{\mathrm{II}}(\alpha, t)[I_t(\alpha, t) - p(\alpha)c_2(\alpha, t)]^2$

Using (A.3), we calculate

(A.12) $I_t(\alpha, t) = \theta_1(\alpha)qZ_2[(1 + t)q]$
  $+ [\theta_2(\alpha)p(\alpha) - \theta_1(\alpha)q]z_{2t}^f(t) + T_t(\alpha, t)$

(A.13) $I_{tt}(\alpha, t) = \theta_1(\alpha)q^2 Z_2{}'[(1 + t)q]$
  $+ [\theta_2(\alpha)p(\alpha) - \theta_1(\alpha)q]z_{2tt}^f(t) + T_{tt}(\alpha, t)$

Take (A.6), (A.7), (A.12), and (A.13), and substitute them into (A.11) to obtain

(A.14) $\hat{v}_{tt}(\alpha, 0) = v_{\mathrm{I}}(\alpha, 0)[p(\alpha)^2 c_{2\mathrm{p}}^c(\alpha, 0) - qp(\alpha)\theta_2 Z_2{}'(q)]$
  $+ v_{\mathrm{II}}(\alpha, 0)[\theta_2(\alpha)p(\alpha) - \theta_1(\alpha)q]^2 [z_{2t}^f(0) - Z_2(q)]^2$
  $+ v_{\mathrm{I}}(\alpha, 0)[\theta_2(\alpha)p(\alpha) - \theta_1(\alpha)q][z_{2tt}^t(0) - qZ_2{}'(q)]$

Take (A.6) and (A.12) and substitute them into (A.9) to obtain

(A.15) $\hat{v}_t(\alpha, 0) = v_I(\alpha, 0)[\theta_2(\alpha)p(\alpha) - \theta_1(\alpha)q][z_{2t}^f(0) - Z_2(q)]$

Since $Ev_{\mathrm{I}}(\alpha, 0)[\theta_2(\alpha)p(\alpha) - \theta_1(\alpha)q] = 0$ for an optimal portfolio choice [see (5.26)], substitution of (A.14) and (A.15) into (A.4) yields

(A.16) $E[\hat{v}(\alpha, t) - \hat{v}(\alpha, 0)] \cong \frac{1}{2}t^2\{Ev_{\mathrm{I}}(\alpha, 0)p(\alpha)[p(\alpha)c_{2\mathrm{p}}^c(\alpha, 0)$
  $- q\theta_2(\alpha)Z_2{}'(q)] + Ev_{\mathrm{II}}(\alpha, 0)[\theta_2(\alpha)p(\alpha)$
  $- \theta_1(\alpha)q]^2 [z_{2t}^f(0) - Z_2(q)]^2\}$

which is (8.15), since at $t = 0$ we have $z_{2t}^f = dz_2/dt$.

Appendix B

Derivation of the Optimal Policies for Section 10.3

We derive here the optimal policy in the presence of a probability of confiscation. The notation is the same as in Chapter 10.

The optimal production pattern and portfolio composition is a solution to the following problem:

(B.1) choose $z_1^L, z_2^L, z_1^F, z_2^F, Z_2$

to maximize

$$\pi Ev[p(\alpha); \theta_1(\alpha)\hat{Z}_1(Z_2) + p(\alpha)\theta_2(\alpha)Z_2] + (1 - \pi)Ev[p_2(\alpha);$$
$$\theta_1(\alpha)(z_1^L + z_1^F) + p(\alpha)\theta_2(\alpha)(z_2^L + z_2^F)]$$

subject to

(i) $q_1^L[\hat{Z}_1(Z_2) - z_1^L] + q_2^L[Z_2 - z_2^L] \geq q_1^F z_1^F + q_2^F z_2^F$

(ii) $\hat{Z}_1(Z_2) \geq z_1^L, \qquad Z_2 \geq z_2^L$

(iii) $z_j^L, z_j^F \geq 0, \qquad j = 1, 2$

The left-hand side of (i) represents proceeds from sales of local equities to foreigners, while the right-hand side of (i) represents spending on foreign equities. One cannot sell more than Z_j real equities of type j

[(ii)] to foreigners, and both local and foreign equity holdings have to be nonnegative [(iii)].

In case of confiscation, local residents receive all the returns on locally produced real equities; this is why only Z_j's appear in the first term of the objective function. In case of no confiscation, the same returns are received on both local and foreign equities of the same type; this is why $z_j^L + z_j^F$ appears in the second term of the objective function.

Denoting by μ the multiplier of (i) and by $\mu_j, j = 1, 2$, the multipliers of (ii), we obtain the following first-order conditions (the complementary slackness conditions are not presented, although we shall use them later):[1]

(B.2) $(1 - \pi)Ev_i(z, \alpha)p_j(\alpha)\theta_j(\alpha) - \mu q_j^L - \mu_j \leq 0, \qquad j = 1, 2$

(B.3) $(1 - \pi)Ev_i(z, \alpha)p_j(\alpha)\theta_j(\alpha) - \mu q_j^F \leq 0, \qquad j = 1, 2$

(B.4) $\pi Ev_i(Z, \alpha)[\theta_1(\alpha)\hat{Z}_1' + p(\alpha)\theta_2(\alpha)]$
$$+ \mu(q_1^L \hat{Z}_1' + q_2^L) + \mu_1 \hat{Z}_1' + \mu_2 = 0$$

and (i)–(iii), where $p_1(\alpha) \equiv 1$ and $p_2(\alpha) \equiv p(\alpha)$. The $v_i(z, \alpha)$ and $v_i(Z, \alpha)$ are the marginal utilities of income in state α when confiscation does not and does take place, respectively. The marginal rate of transformation between Z_1 and Z_2 is $- \hat{Z}_1'$.

First, observe that the home country should not sell both types of real equities to foreigners. Suppose it does so; then (ii) is satisfied with strict inequalities, and $\mu_1 = \mu_2 = 0$. Since $q_j^F > q_j^L$, this implies that (B.3) holds with strict inequality for $j = 1, 2$, implying $z_1^F = z_2^F = 0$ (the complimentary slackness condition). This in turn implies that (i) holds with strict inequality which means that $\mu = 0$. But (B.3) cannot hold for $\mu = 0$, a contradiction. Hence, $z_1^L = \hat{Z}_1(Z_2)$ and/or $z_2^L = Z_2$. Without loss of generality, we assume that $z_2^L = Z_2$, which means that the second industry is owned entirely by local residents. Now if, in addition, $z_1^L = \hat{Z}_1(Z_2)$, then there is no trade in securities. This is a possible solution, but we shall concentrate on the more interesting case in which trade in securities does take place. Hence, we assume

$$*z_2^L = *Z_2$$
$$*z_1^L < \hat{Z}_1(*Z_2)$$

----

[1] We assume an interior solution for Z_2 which is in fact constrained to be $0 \leq Z_2 \leq \max\{Z_2 | \hat{Z}_1(Z_2) \geq 0\}$.

where asterisks indicate optimal values. From an argument which is similar to that showing that $z_1{}^L < \hat{Z}_1(Z_2)$ and $z_2{}^L < Z_2$ is not a possible solution, one can show that in the present case

$$*z_1{}^L > 0$$
$$*z_1{}^F = 0$$
$$*z_2{}^F > 0$$

which means that the country is not buying abroad equities of the type that it sells to foreigners (type 1); it buys from foreigners equities of the other type, those issued by the industry that it fully owns; and it owns part of the industry whose equities are exported.

This solution implies the following binding conditions from (B.2) and (B.3):

(B.2a) $$\qquad\qquad (1 - \pi)Ev_{\mathrm{l}}(*z, \alpha)\theta_1(\alpha) - *\mu q_1{}^L = 0$$

(B.2b) $$\qquad (1 - \pi)Ev_{\mathrm{l}}(*z, \alpha)p(\alpha)\theta_2(\alpha) - *\mu q_2{}^L - *\mu_2 = 0$$

(B.3a) $$\qquad (1 - \pi)Ev_{\mathrm{l}}(*z, \alpha)p(\alpha)\theta_2(\alpha) - *\mu q_2{}^F = 0$$

with $*\mu > 0$ and $*\mu_1 = 0$.

From (B.2b) and (B.3a), we obtain

(B.5) $$\qquad\qquad *\mu_2 = *\mu(q_2{}^F - q_2{}^L) > 0$$

Substituting (B.5) into (B.4) and solving for $-\hat{Z}_1'\,(= \mathrm{MRT})$, we obtain

(B.6) $$\qquad \mathrm{MRT} = -*\hat{Z}_1' = \frac{\pi Ev_{\mathrm{l}}(*Z, \alpha)p(\alpha)\theta_2(\alpha) + *\mu q_2{}^F}{\pi Ev_{\mathrm{l}}(*Z, \alpha)\theta_1(\alpha) + *\mu q_1{}^L}$$

In case $\pi = 0$ (that is, there is no danger of confiscation), $\mathrm{MRT} = q_2{}^F/q_1{}^L$. But in this case, $q_j{}^L = q_j{}^F = q_j$ for $j = 1, 2$, and we obtain the result from Chapters 5 and 6.

Using (B.2a) and (B.2b), we can also write (B.6) in the form

(B.7) $$\qquad \mathrm{MRT} = -*\hat{Z}_1'$$

$$= \frac{E[\pi v_{\mathrm{l}}(*Z, \alpha) + (1 - \pi)v_{\mathrm{l}}(*z, \alpha)]p(\alpha)\theta_2(\alpha)}{E[\pi v_{\mathrm{l}}(*Z, \alpha) + (1 - \pi)v_{\mathrm{l}}(*z, \alpha)]\theta_1(\alpha)}$$

which is similar to (5.23) (with $-\hat{Z}_1' = q$), but here the marginal utilities of income are a weighted average of the marginal utilities in case of confiscation and no confiscation, where the weights are the corresponding probabilities.

Suppose, for the moment, that the optimal production point has been chosen. Let us see how a market economy can achieve an optimal portfolio composition.

The investor's problem is given by

(B.8)   choose $z_1{}^L, z_2{}^L, z_1{}^F, z_2{}^F$

to maximize

$$\pi Ev[p(\alpha); \theta_1(\alpha)z_1{}^L + p(\alpha)\theta_2(\alpha)z_2{}^L + T(\alpha)] + (1 - \pi)Ev[p(\alpha);$$
$$\theta_1(\alpha)(z_1{}^L + z_1{}^F) + p(\alpha)\theta_2(\alpha)(z_2{}^L + z_2{}^F)]$$

subject to

(i) $g_1z_1{}^L + g_2z_2{}^L + g_1{}^Fz_1{}^F + q_2{}^Fz_2{}^F \leq Y$

(ii) $z_1{}^L, z_2{}^L, z_1{}^F, z_2{}^F \geq 0$

where g is a consumer price, and (since we have one degree of freedom in the choice of prices) we have chosen $g_2{}^F = q_2{}^F$; that is, we have chosen $z_2{}^F$ as the untaxed security; Y is net wealth, and it equals the value of (Z_1, Z_2) at producer prices in terms of the numeraire, minus net taxes or transfers imposed on or distributed by the government; and $T(\alpha)$ is the lump-sum transfer defined in (10.11).

Denoting by λ the multiplier of (i), we obtain the following first-order conditions for the consumer problem:

(B.9) $\pi Ev_1(1, \alpha)p_j(\alpha)\theta_j(\alpha)$

$$+ (1 - \pi)Ev_1(2, \alpha)p_j(\alpha)\theta_j(\alpha) - \lambda g_j \leq 0, \qquad j = 1, 2$$

(B.10) $(1 - \pi)Ev_1(2, \alpha)\theta_1(\alpha) - \lambda g_1{}^F \leq 0$

(B.11) $(1 - \pi)Ev_1(2, \alpha)p(\alpha)\theta_2(\alpha) - \lambda q_2{}^F \leq 0$

and (i)–(ii). $v_1(1, \alpha)$ is the marginal utility of income in state α in case of confiscation, while $v_1(2, \alpha)$ is the marginal utility of income in state α if confiscation does not take place.

The optimal values of the decision variables are given by

$$Z_2 = {}^*Z_2 > 0$$
$$z_1{}^L = {}^*z_1{}^L > 0$$
$$z_2{}^L = {}^*Z_2 > 0$$
$$z_1{}^F = {}^*z_1{}^F = 0$$
$$z_2{}^F = {}^*z_2{}^F > 0$$
$$v_1(1, \alpha) = v_1({}^*Z, \alpha)$$
$$v_1(2, \alpha) = v_1({}^*z, \alpha)$$

Substituting these values into (B.9)–(B.11), we obtain (using the complementary slackness conditions)

(B.9a) $\pi E v_1(^*Z, \alpha) p_j(\alpha) \theta_j(\alpha)$
$$+ (1 - \pi) E v_1(^*z, \alpha) p_j(\alpha) \theta_j(\alpha) - {}^*\lambda g_j = 0, \qquad j = 1, 2$$

(B.10a) $$(1 - \pi) E v_1(^*z, \alpha) \theta_1(\alpha) - {}^*\lambda g_1^{\mathrm{F}} \leq 0$$

(B.11a) $$(1 - \pi) E v_1(^*z, \alpha) p(\alpha) \theta_2(\alpha) - {}^*\lambda q_2^{\mathrm{F}} = 0$$

By comparing (B.11a) with (B.3a), we get

(B.12) $$^*\lambda = {}^*\mu$$

In this case, a comparison of (B.10a) with (B.3), using (B.12), reveals that there is no need to tax purchases of foreign type-1 securities. Hence, we choose

(B.13) $$g_1^{\mathrm{F}} = q_1^{\mathrm{F}}$$

By comparing (B.9a) with (B.2a) and (B.3a), using (B.12), we obtain

(B.14) $$g_1 - q_1^{\mathrm{L}} = \frac{1}{^*\mu} \pi E v_1(^*Z, \alpha) \theta_1(\alpha)$$

(B.15) $$g_2 - q_2^{\mathrm{F}} = \frac{1}{^*\mu} \pi E v_1(^*Z, \alpha) p(\alpha) \theta_2(\alpha)$$

Now, let d_j be the price of equity j that a local producer receives. Then, if we choose

(B.16) $$d_j = \frac{1}{^*\mu} E[\pi v_1(^*Z, \alpha) + (1 - \pi) v_1(^*z, \alpha)] p_j(\alpha) \theta_j(\alpha)$$
$$j = 1, 2$$

it is clear from (B.7) that the optimal production point will be chosen. In addition, by comparing (B.16) with (B.9a), using (B.12), we have

(B.17) $$g_j = d_j, \qquad j = 1, 2$$

Hence, producer prices should be the same as investor prices.
    Let

(B.18) $$\mathrm{sub}_j = \frac{1}{^*\mu} \pi E v_1(^*Z, \alpha) p_j(\alpha) \theta_j(\alpha), \qquad j = 1, 2$$

Then from (B.13)–(B.17), we get the optimal price structure

(B.19) $$d_1 = g_1 = q_1{}^L + \text{sub}_1$$

(B.20) $$d_2 = g_2 = q_2{}^F + \text{sub}_2$$

(B.21) $$g_1{}^F = q_1{}^F$$

(B.22) $$g_2{}^F = q_2{}^F \qquad \text{(numeraire)}$$

It is now easy to see what the optimal taxation policy should be. The government should provide a subsidy on equity exports. The subsidy should be sub_1 per real equity of type 1. The wedge between $g_2 (= d_2)$ and $q_2{}^F$ will be generated by market forces, since s_2 also expresses the premium that the private sector puts at the margin on $z_2{}^L$ over $z_2{}^F$ [compare (B.11a) with (B.9a) for $j = 2$].

Index

A

Anderson, J., 54, 55, 85
Arrow, K. J., 28, 29, 31, 35, 63
Arrow securities, 33–35

B

Balance of payments, 79, 86, 160, 162
Balance of trade, 83, 88, *see also* Trade account
Baldwin, R. E., 141
Bardhan, P. K., 44, 45
Batra, R. N., 44–46, 55–57
Bellman's principle of optimality, 159
Bhagwati, J., 150
Brainard, W. C., 43, 44–46

C

Capital account, 85, 160, 162
Cass, D., 31, 153
Caves, R. E., 5
Cobb–Douglas, 52, 101, 102, 143, 146, 147, 171
Commercial policy, 3, 109, *see also* Tariff
Comparative advantage, 12, 52, 58, 94, 96, 97, 99, 162
Comparative costs theory, 5, 94, *see also* Ricardian theory
Comparative disadvantage, 51, 96
Complete markets, 35, 39, 63
Confiscation risk, 149
Contingent commodity markets, 32, 39, 58, 85
Cooper, R. N., 43–46
Corden, W. M., 109
Current account, 160, 162

D

Das, S. K., 56
Diamond, P. A., 64–66

E

Ekern, S., 66, 122
Equity
  subsidy, 117, 140
  tax, 139, 140, 142, 143, 145–147
Ethier, W., 94
Ex-ante trading decision, 44, 48, 49, 61
Ex-post trading decision, 44, 50, 61

F

Factor movement, 102, 142, 143
Factor price equalization, 20, 56, 58, 94,
    99, 100, 102, 162, 168
Future market, 63, 89

G

Gains from trade, 3, 127, 128, 130–137

H

Hanoch, G., 46
Hart, O. D., 64, 137
Heckscher, E., 13
Heckscher–Ohlin
    model, 22, 55, 57, 64, 74, 75, 102, 103,
        117, 162
    theorem, 24, 26, 94, 106, 107
    theory, 5, 13, 15, 26, 99
Helpman, E., 61, 66
Hicks composite, 160

I

Incomplete markets, 39, 40, 137
Increasing risk, 31

J

Jones, R. W., 5, 19, 21, 24, 94, 142

K

Kemp, M. C., 2, 5, 22, 45, 46, 50, 51, 58,
    70, 85, 142, 149
Keynes, J. M., 149

L

Liviatan, N., 50, 51, 58, 70, 85

M

Magnification effect, 19, 21
Markowitz, H. M., 1
Mayer, W., 57, 58
Mean-preserving spread, 55
Metzler, L. A., 111
Metzler paradox, 111
Monopoly power, 139, 141–143, 151
Morgenstern, O., 27
Mundell, R. A., 102

O

Ohlin, B., 13, 24
Ohyama, M., 45, 46

P

Pomery, J. G., 58, 61
Pratt, J. W., 28, 31

R

Razin, A., 61, 66
Ricardian
    model, 13, 16, 50, 64, 73–75, 162
    theory, 5, 13, 15
Ricardo, D., 5, 6
Riley, J. G., 54, 55, 85
Risk aversion
    absolute, 28–31, 56
    relative, 28, 29, 31
Risk premium, 56, 58
Rothschild, M., 31
Ruffin, R. J., 44, 47, 48, 50, 51, 85
Russell, W. R., 44–46
Rybczynski, T. M., 20
Rybczynski theorem, 21, 23, 56, 58, 94,
    105, 106, 162

S

Samuelson, P. A., 10, 19, 20
Sandmo, A., 56
Scheinkman, J. A., 94
Service account, 85, 87, 160
Spanning condition, 122
Srinivasan, T. N., 150
Stiglitz, J. E., 31, 153, 168
Stolper, W. F., 19
Stolper–Samuelson theorem, 19, 21, 24,
    25, 56, 58, 94, 103–105, 114, 117, 162

T

Tariff, 2, 109–113, 115–123, 125, 133,
    134, 136, 142, 143, 145–147
    optimal, 139, 151
Tobin, J., 1
Trade account, 84–86, 88, 160, *see also*
    Balance of trade
Turnovsky, S. J., 50, 51, 85

V

von Neumann, J., 27
von Neumann–Morgenstern utility func-
    tion, 32, 44, 70, 157

W

Wilson, R., 66, 122

ECONOMIC THEORY, ECONOMETRICS, AND MATHEMATICAL ECONOMICS

Consulting Editor: Karl Shell

UNIVERSITY OF PENNSYLVANIA
PHILADELPHIA, PENNSYLVANIA

Franklin M. Fisher and Karl Shell. The Economic Theory of Price Indices: *Two Essays on the Effects of Taste, Quality, and Technological Change*

Luis Eugenio Di Marco (Ed.). International Economics and Development: *Essays in Honor of Raúl Presbisch*

Erwin Klein. Mathematical Methods in Theoretical Economics: *Topological and Vector Space Foundations of Equilibrium Analysis*

Paul Zarembka (Ed.). Frontiers in Econometrics

George Horwich and Paul A. Samuelson (Eds.). Trade, Stability, and Macroeconomics: *Essays in Honor of Lloyd A. Metzler*

W. T. Ziemba and R. G. Vickson (Eds.). Stochastic Optimization Models in Finance

Steven A. Y. Lin (Ed.). Theory and Measurement of Economic Externalities

David Cass and Karl Shell (Eds.). The Hamiltonian Approach to Dynamic Economics

R. Shone. Microeconomics: *A Modern Treatment*

C. W. J. Granger and Paul Newbold. Forecasting Economic Time Series

Michael Szenberg, John W. Lombardi, and Eric Y. Lee. Welfare Effects of Trade Restrictions: *A Case Study of the U.S. Footwear Industry*

Haim Levy and Marshall Sarnat (Eds.). Financial Decision Making under Uncertainty

Yasuo Murata. Mathematics for Stability and Optimization of Economic Systems

Alan S. Blinder and Philip Friedman (Eds.). Natural Resources, Uncertainty, and General Equilibrium Systems: *Essays in Memory of Rafael Lusky*

Jerry S. Kelly. Arrow Impossibility Theorems

Peter Diamond and Michael Rothschild (Eds.). Uncertainty in Economics: *Readings and Exercises*

Fritz Machlup. Methodology of Economics and Other Social Sciences

Robert H. Frank and Richard T. Freeman. Distributional Consequences of Direct Foreign Investment

Elhanan Helpman and Assaf Razin. **A Theory of International Trade Under Uncertainty**

Edmund S. Phelps (Ed.). **Studies in Macroeconomic Theory, Volume 1:** *Employment and Inflation*

In preparation

Marc Nerlove, David M. Grether, and José L. Carvalho. **Analysis of Economic Time Series:** *A Synthesis*

Thomas J. Sargent. **Macroeconomic Theory**

Michael J. Boskin (Ed.). **Economics and Human Welfare:** *Essays in Honor of Tibor Scitovsky*

A 8
B 9
C 0
D 1
E 2
F 3
G 4
H 5
I 6
J 7